Out Of The Shadows

My Autobiography

Hazel Helliwell

Bannister Publications Ltd
118 Saltergate
Chesterfield
S40 1NG

First published in Great Britain in 2011 by

Bannister Publications Ltd
118 Saltergate
Chesterfield
Derbyshire S40 1NG

ISBN 978-0-9566196-3-1

A catalogue record for this book is available from the British Library

Typeset in Platino Linotype
Cover design by The Kabin Design Ltd, Chesterfield, Derbyshire
Printed and bound in Great Britain by the
MPG Books Group, Bodmin and King's Lynn

MPG Books Ltd, Bodmin, Cornwall

Other books by Hazel Helliwell under the pen name of
Samantha Arran:

Love Never Fails
Unfailing Love
A New Beginning
Jason and Marigold

Love Never Fails, hardback, £7.99, *Unfailing Love* and *Jason and Marigold* both paper back £6.99, published by AH Stockwell Ltd (www.ahstockwell.co.uk) and obtainable from the publishers, Amazon, Waterstones, W.H. Smith, Blackwell and other good book shops.

A New Beginning, paper back £7.99, published by Bannister Publications Ltd, Chesterfield, and available from the publisher at 118 Saltergate, Chesterfield S40 ING. Tel. 01246 550488. (Open Monday to Friday), or from Amazon, Waterstones and by order through any bookshop.

Foreword

This story of my life is a reflection on the power and unconditional love of Jesus as in faith I trust in him.

After completion I began to feel stronger in every way. It has been very therapeutic for me.

This book is dedicated to all who persevere.

Grateful thanks to my sister Marie for the loan of photographs from our mother's collection. Also grateful thanks to the Dowager Duchess of Devonshire, for allowing me to use her photograph.

The proceeds from this book will be donated to Churches Together Dronfield & District for Outreach and Mission. N.S.P.C.C.

Chapter 1

There was a little girl who had a little curl right in the middle of her forehead. When she was good she was very, very good but when she was bad, she was horrid.

I hadn't a little curl in the middle of my forehead. I had fluffy white hair which only curled Sunday mornings for Sunday school; and only then because on Saturday evenings my mother nearly pulled my hair out when putting in rag rollers. But I was very, very good – I daren't be otherwise.

I was the seventh child. My sister Gladys was the first born, then Ernest who died as a baby, Albert, Hilda, Jack, Hugh was two years older than me, and then Marie, who is five years younger. Mother had Marie when she was 'in the change of life', as it was called then. Our maiden name is Crossley.

I can't recall many memories in my first four years, just snatches. I vividly remember before I was five years we moved into a new house, 227 Sheffield Road, Unstone Green, part of the council estate which had been built around that time. Before then, we had lived at Old Whittington before moving into a large static caravan – every drop of water had to be carried – it must have been very hard for my mother and Gladys. Nearby was another caravan where Mr and Mrs Purdy lived and there was a fish and chip shop owned by Mr and Mrs Paling. I can't remember having fish and chips from there. They also had a small farm.

How we came to be living in the caravan isn't part of my story. As Gladys, at 95 years and still highly intelligent and 'bright as a button' as we say, has told me several times, "it's better for me not to know". That is good enough for me. I leave it there, out of respect for her. However, she told me about great grandma Harriet who was very kind and gentle and a real lady, and whom I am told I resemble in looks and manner. I wish I had known her. I remember my maternal grandma Wright very well. She lived in Eckington and brought me buttons, which I liked to play with, and we visited her.

I must have been five or six when, waking up on Christmas morning, I saw a small blue wooden bed with a pale blue quilt with a bow and a pillow, also with a bow and both made from the same material. Gladys had made them and lying in the bed was a beautifully dressed doll with mother's knitting.

Someone in our family has a photograph of me standing with a big doll's pram and a doll. I had a fringe and a big floppy ribbon tied at the side of my head. Albert had turned the dolls head to face the camera!

My father was very cruel to my mother and to my three older brothers. We all were like 'zombies', afraid to move, especially at the table. He didn't hit me but he would hit my mother when he was frustrated. No child should grow up in that atmosphere. My father was 30 years older than my mother and had been a sergeant major in the First World War, after which he owned a small pottery works at Sheepbridge. My mother and her mother, Granny Wright, worked for him. His grandfather had been the Mayor of Birmingham and his wife was called Harriet. Father's sister was named Emily and she and her husband Samuel lived in Harrogate. Samuel had a fine Brougham open carriage, led by two beautiful black horses with plumes on their heads, in which drove the aristocracy around the parks for sightseeing and on other occasions. Father had five sons from his first marriage but all died in infancy; when Ernest died he thought this was happening again.

My mother was an only child and had never known her father. Her mother had been spiteful and cruel to her. My mother's right eye had been burnt when she 'fell' onto the coal fire bar, so she had no eyelid and always had a red lower lid.

❧

I remember all of us spending nights in the air raid shelters at the back of Unstone main road school, when Sheffield suffered the long nights of the 'blitz'. I was very young but was able to begin knitting a blue scarf for an airman. With no sleep, Hugh and I went to school and the few teachers there were surprised we had turned up. They sent us home to bed. The next morning during assembly, our headmaster Mr Sharman told the school that Hugh and I had come the previous morning with shining clean faces and well brushed hair!

When we were growing up, we were kept spotlessly clean using red Lifebuoy soap. We were sturdy and well fed. Most days we completed our hot meal with a suet pudding. When I was in the kitchen I used to watch my mother wrapping the pudding in a big spotless white cloth, closing the top with string, then putting it into a pan of boiling water. We always had sweet white sauce with spotted dick. The home-made rice puddings were gorgeous, made in the small oven at the side of the coal fire. I have often wondered how my mother timed her bread and cakes and other dishes in the big oven heated by the fire. There were no temperature gauges in those days, but everything turned out perfect.

One morning as I was sitting in front of the fire, my brother Jack put the poker into the coals to heat and then ran it over the front of his shoes and boots to make them shine. Albert and Jack were very well groomed – Jack in particular – I suppose you would call him 'a ladies man' My mother boiled their white shirts and starched the collars and cuffs. Jack spent ages getting a crease in his trousers with the flat iron, for there were no electric irons then; he was very particular. Hugh was very clean but dressed more casually.

Marie, always mischievous and curious, got hold of the poker and because it was hot, let go. It landed on my left leg just above the knee. I still have a three-inch scar there. Father used to dress it and when he pulled the old dressing off, "Ouch!", it hurt.

Father was always kind to me and took me to Chesterfield pictures also the theatre and short walks. I reminded him of his former wife's daughter, Ethel, who was married to a Cooperative manager some miles away from us. My mother travelled on two buses to go to clean for her. Whatever did she think? Most likely she just accepted that it was something she had to do.

৯

I vividly remember when I was six or seven years old and, dressed in a beautiful new knee length coat, I called for my friend Jean to show her my new coat before we all set off for Sunday school. Their little terrier dog was sitting on the path as usual and, for no reason other than perhaps my new coat, he bit the back of my left leg. Frightened, I startled the family by bursting into their kitchen. I can't remember much else only that my father went down to see them. I still have a scar. One day when I went to see Jean and her brother Jack, their father had bought them each a very small leather armchair and on the arm was a chocolate Kit-Kat bar. Although we were well fed and well clothed, we never had luxuries like that in our house.

৯

Because Albert was older than me I missed my father's cruelty him, but was later told that he screamed when father took off his belt. I was also told that father had been so pleased to have a son after Ernest died that he had spoilt Albert, and then knocked all this out of him. There was always a cane at the fireside and my three brothers had permanent marks on the backs of their knees where they had been caned. One morning when I was very young I saw him hit my mother in the mouth with the side of his hand as she was ironing. As he walked away I remember her saying, "There, she has seen you now".

Once, as we were seated round the table, he hit Marie on the top of her head with the flat part of the carving knife – she was only two years old. Mother cried "Oh, no, not her". He picked up his beaker of tea and asked her, "Do you want this in your face? You're ugly enough now, but will be uglier still when I have finished with you".

Before breakfast one morning my brother Hugh and I were in the front room and he was messing around, teasing me. It was nothing harmful. Our father came in and hit him. Hugh ran to the door to get out, followed by father; he sank down and was kicked several times. During breakfast Hugh was frightened and crying. Father said, "If you don't stop snivelling, you'll get some more". Hugh instantly froze. I still weep at this memory.

We were all strong and healthy except for Marie, who suffered every childhood illness going. It was annoying that Hugh and I had to stay off school whilst she was infectious. Marie and I shared the same bed, as children often did in those days, but I never caught anything!

Always mischievous, Marie often got into trouble at school with her friends. I intervened when their older sisters got on to her and I had a fist fight with one of them; then our teacher, Mrs Draycott, made me stay in after school. Our playground was segregated from the boys.

Marie was mother's favourite, although she was often a pain to me. I had to take her everywhere, but she was a little love with her big blue eyes and her beautiful hands with long fingers and nails. Even today, Marie still has her big beautiful blue eyes and lovely hands – she takes pride in her nails and goes to the manicurist.

❧

What we all dreaded at school was the 'Nit Nurse' coming to examine us. I must have had some because mother combed some thick stuff, smelling of disinfectant, through my hair.

Even when we were very young all my friends and I would spend our school holidays by the side of Unstone Green River, where we girls would make 'houses' with a circle of white stones. We took along any small pieces of rugs we could find, bottles of water and home-made bread and jam, and played with our dolls and prams and dolls' tea sets.

The boys climbed up to the railway line to watch the passing trains or they swam in the river. One day we had the excitement of Sidney having his thumb bitten by a squirrel. It wouldn't let go! It was a time of innocence and we made our own amusements. There was no television then but we listened to the radio. Sitting round the table at home we made rag rugs, pegging on to sackcloth pieces of material cut from old coats or stuff we could get from jumble sales.

Hugh and I had to go to St Mary's church from school twice a week to clean it. I was only seven years old and Hugh was nine. We had to sweep the church and wash the long aisle. Occasionally we had to black lead the long heating pipes than ran all round the church just above the floor. Albert and Jack fed the big boiler under the church with coke and coal.

ॐ

Our parents were not married and in those days I suppose it was thought of as a disgrace. No-one at school dared say anything to my brothers; and girls and boys had segregated playgrounds in those days. Each time the teacher held my book up as an example of neat writing I would be taunted by my 'friends', "Who do you think you are?" I suppose it could have been a lot worse but insecurity plagued me. Also, when my brothers had been beaten by our father and at the odd times when mother hit me for no reason, I can only say that when someone hits you, you feel unloved. How did my mother cope? Most likely all she could do was, like all of us, get on with our lives but....

I was seven years old when I was told by my friends at school that my parents had got married. No-one in the family told me but it was the truth.

When we could, after school and on Saturday mornings, all the children from the Green went into the wood, taking old prams and anything we had with wheels to collect firewood from the trees that were being chopped down. The mature chestnut trees were cut down to make pit props. I can still smell the scent of the felled trees. I loved to get hold of some of the large chippings that had been chopped out from where the big axes had weakened the trees so they would fall down before being sawn up for logs. We collected all the kindling wood. I once took home a bundle of sticks I thought would also be perfect to light the fire. A neighbour came – I had taken his pea sticks! He was laughing and good-natured about it.

(I was told recently that, interestingly, Pearson's Potteries of Whittington Moor owned the land; their clay pits were there but the clay was running out. Pearson Potteries wanted to build houses on the land but were refused permission. A ski slope was mentioned but was also turned down. However, a golf course was accepted. As the clay pits were filled in, people would throw in all kinds of rubbish, including dead dogs.)

On Saturday afternoons we all walked to the Lyceum cinema at Whittington Moor for the matinee. We were pelted with orange peel and apple cores from the balcony!

Neville Briggs was one of our gang. I called for him one morning, to find his grandmother sitting on a kitchen chair just inside the back door, crying and Neville's mum grumbling at her. Neville was standing at the side of his grandmother with his arm around her shoulders. The loving kindness of Neville is embedded in my mind

I blancoed my white summer shoes and put these on the window sill to dry. Walking to Sunday school we used to step on the big gas tar bubbles to burst them. Not good on white shoes! I haven't seen gas tar bubbles for years. We always had a drink of Tizer or Dandelion and Burdock with our Sunday roast lunch, then at teatime the ice cream van came and we took a cup for him to fill.

༃

My mother took me on the buses when I was eight years old to help my stepsister Ethel for a week, by taking her three-year-old grandson Anthony in his push chair for walks as his parents had gone on holiday. Iris, Anthony's mother, and Ethel knew I had looked after Marie. They lived in a lovely big detached house.

Mother went home and Anthony showed me his tractors and I read him a story until Ethel told me to wash my hands ready for lunch. She said I was to call her 'Aunt Ethel', and that I had to keep Anthony out for three hours every morning and afternoon. I thought, 'What if it rains?' We had salad and cold meat but no bread and butter, then fruit. I was still hungry. That week is imprinted deeply in my mind.

With Anthony in his push chair we went along a quiet lane that Aunt Ethel had directed me to. The hedges were showing promise of big blackberries and we almost went as far as Hardwick Hall. Anthony chatted to me and I kept stopping so he could watch the birds and aeroplanes and see rabbits running in the fields. He told me when he wanted to 'wee-wee'.

When we returned, 'Uncle' Robert and my step-niece Marcia had come home from work. Marcia worked in Chesterfield at John Turner's shop. We had a hot meal, serving ourselves from tureens – Aunt Ethel was very dignified and posh. We then had a biscuit and cheese but I was still hungry.

Aunt Ethel said to me, "Do you eat like this at home? You eat too much." I started crying and asked,

"May I go home, please?" I thought she was going to starve me. I remember this vividly. Marcia cuddled me and told her mother "She is only eight years old and still growing, I can feel her bones. When I was her age I was never full." Aunt Ethel fetched a plate of bread and jam and a glass of milk. I told her, "We have a big pudding and custard after our meal at home." She answered, "You are a big family." Aunt Ethel promised to make me a pudding every day and then asked if I was still hungry. "Yes, Aunt Ethel." I really was, I wasn't being greedy. She brought me some biscuits, cheese and a glass of milk and I thanked her.

Marcia promised me, "We'll look after you Hazel. Tomorrow morning we will all go to church and then after lunch I can come walking with you and Anthony and I can show you some walks to do during the week. On Wednesday I have the afternoon free, so I could take you both up to the village and call to see you dad." He agreed and I thanked them. Uncle Robert said that I was well mannered. They didn't ask any questions about my home life.

I also remember that I was excited at going out with Marcia. We slept in the same bed and I had to use a stool to climb up onto her high bed with its big feather mattress. She was beautiful and later she became engaged to a soldier who was aboard. Whenever I was in Chesterfield I regularly went to see Marcia; she was always smiling and smelt lovely.

The sun shone all that week and I really enjoyed myself. Mother fetched me home on Saturday afternoon and Aunt Ethel told her I had been very good and helpful. She gave my mother some money and she kissed me.

࿇

When I was eight, I started knitting skirts for myself and for Marie. Mother put a cotton bodice on the skirts and knitted jumpers to match. Our home made dresses and matching ribbons were starched, as were my brother's shirt collars and cuffs. My mother also washed, starched and ironed the surplices for the church choir. Her washing was immaculate and the whites were 'whiter than white'. She would line the wicker clothes basket with pages of the Derbyshire Times and I never understood why the print didn't come off.

࿇

Jack was engaged to be married to a beautiful girl. I loved her and her family but he met Violet with bright ginger hair and he broke off the engagement. I had my bridesmaid dress, head dress, shoes and socks all ready for the wedding. I was heartbroken to lose this family. I had asked my friend Audrey be a bridesmaid with me – we were the same size – and she was excited at the prospect. However, mother shortened our dresses and Audrey and I were able to wear them for Sunday school, and we wore our shoes for school.

࿇

Our Sunday school went to Bridlington for the day. It seemed that the coach took days to get there, so eager were we to see the sea. Mrs Naden, our choir mistress, invited me to go with her for a boat ride. Hugh was standing alone and I was not going without him but we had spent our pocket money. As I started to get off the boat Mrs Naden asked me where I was going. I told her Hugh hadn't any money so she paid for him. We had a wonderful, unforgettable day.

❧

When I was 11 years old, I went back to Aunt Ethel's for a week in the summer holiday to take Anthony out and about. Surprisingly, she told me to call her 'Ethel' and she fed me well! We couldn't go far without Anthony's pushchair but we walked and sat in the fields. We read to each other; he played with his toys and we chased about. I took him to the local swings and we spent time in Ethel's garden. Marcia wasn't there – she had married her fiancée and lived in London. We hadn't been invited to the wedding.

❧

I can't remember my mother discussing the 'facts of life' with me but Gladys told me about it.

❧

I used to go for walks with father we would sit on a bench at Unstone Green as he smoked his pipe. I have searched my memory but can't recall any conversations we may have had. Father died when he was 84 years old and I was 12. Father had been a violinist and had played at the Chesterfield Hippodrome theatre, now called the Pomegranate. When he was practising at home, people passing by thought a lady was singing. Jack was also very talented at playing his accordion.

❧

In the summer holidays we often walked up to Dronfield Cliffe Park with a bottle of water and sandwiches. We went on the see-saw, swings and roundabout. We avoided Friday afternoons when the furnaces from the works on Calleywhite Lane were cleaned out, making black smoke that descended on the park and the sour smell was terrible. That all ended when the country went 'smokeless'.

In those days we had a week off school in October for potato picking. A gang of us went to a farm at Hundall and I remember that as we walked up to the farm we experimented with cigarettes that we had made with pieces of rag rolled in newspaper. We only did that three times! At lunch time the farmer's wife brought us big white jugs of cocoa and hot chocolate and we drank it, sitting on a hay stack and eating our home-made bread and jam. She gave each of us a big potato to take home every tea-time and we were paid on the Saturday morning. I was always happy taking home the big potato.

Hugh and I had a miniature printing set that we both loved. I can't remember where it came from. We put small letters in a gadget of three lines with tweezers then stamped this on to a pad we had inked, then on to paper.

❧

When I was 12, I began to deliver the morning papers for Mr Walker at Unstone. I walked over the hill to collect the bag and delivered to Siscar Cottage before going on to Ranshaw Lodge and through the wood to the side of the river and waterfall before delivering at

Mill House, then up the Red lane to Unstone Green. I loved these early mornings. I have always been an early morning person: early to bed and early to rise.

It was wonderful walking through the wood, sniffing its woody, earthy perfume and the smell of ochre from the waterfall. In the autumn the lingering aromas from the previous evening's garden fires filled the air. Watching the birds and listening to them, seeing the squirrels chasing about, I didn't know fear of being alone, for we could walk anywhere without getting into danger.

I was now one of the senior girls at school and on Friday afternoons we went to clean the air raid shelters. The war was over of course, but the shelters got flooded and needed to be swept out. When it was one of our birthdays we had a party. One time we tried to make custard heated by a candle and very bravely ate the cold lumpy result – "Ughh!" Despite this we had good and innocent times

Miss Pamela Cooper from Mill House would let me ride her horse in the school holidays. She also gave me her saved 'Girl's Crystal' magazines. After playing in the wood and on the disused railway line, walking past their home, her dad gave us the biggest cooking apples from his tree. Mrs Cooper was an accomplished pianist and I loved to hear her play.

Before Christmas we would sit at the kitchen table making paper chains, gluing them together for decorating. Gladys made flowers from melted wax and stuck them on to small twigs for vases.

∾

I have often had regrets since my childhood days. Could I have talked to father about his cruelty to my brothers and mother? But would this have made it worse? Would it have undermined his authority? Would my family have resented my being able to converse with him when they were not allowed? So many questions and there is only one answer: give all this to Jesus and ask for all of us to be healed into victory over the memories and damage. When these doubts rear their ugly heads I think of the love of Jesus that Miss Barber taught us about.

ھ

Every summer the Church and Unstone Chapel held the Whitsuntide Walk, following a decorated lorry. Marie and I always had a new decorated straw bonnet to wear and after this walk we all enjoyed the Chapel tea party.

I have said many, many times, I don't know what we would have done without our Sunday school teacher, Miss Roberta Barber of Hounscliffe, Unstone Green. She was so gentle and loving and she taught us about Jesus and his love. She played the organ in St Mary's Church at Unstone and my brothers took it in turn to pump the air bellows. Jack kept falling asleep so she couldn't play! We were in the choir stalls and had to wake him up.

When we were aged 12, the Christian girls were confirmed at St John's Church, Dronfield, on 24 June 1945. Gladys bought me my white dress and I can picture it now – knee length and in a silky material with small gathers down each side to the waist, and short sleeves. Miss Barber gave each of us a book in remembrance of the occasion, 'Just For Me – Help for Young Disciples' by Laura A. Barter Snow. My book is almost worn out, for there aren't many days when I haven't read the prayers and verses in it. It is very precious to me because Miss Barber gave it to me.

છ

I left school at 14 and from Monday to Saturday I went to live in Hundall with our church choir mistress, Mrs Naden, her husband and daughter Mary. My job was to clean the house and help Mrs Naden, who taught the piano at home. I was happy. We all ate together and I slept with Mary, who was a few months older than me. Mary was lovely, tall like her dad, with blue eyes and fair hair that was full of waves; her mother had wavy curling hair, but dark brown. Mary went privately to Dronfield Grammar School, later renamed Henry Fanshawe School. Her dad was a business man. He had to travel occasionally and one time when he had been to Scotland he brought back for Mary two hand-knitted sets of a Fair Isle beret with matching scarf and gloves, one beige and one blue.

One Friday afternoon I was feeling homesick and asked Mrs Naden if I may go home and return the next morning to do the Saturday work. She was playing her piano and I remember her looking anxious. She asked if there was anything wrong and I assured her that I just wanted to go home. When I turned up unexpectedly at home with my wages, my mother asked me to go to Whittington Moor for fish and chips. It was the first time she had asked me to do this.

I caught the bus for Whittington Moor and saw a school friend who told me that Mr Taylor and Mr McCall, the headmasters of the main road and church schools, were upstairs. I was very shy in those days but I went upstairs and sat near them. They were deep in conversation but when he saw me, Mr Taylor asked how I was. He went on to say that he and Mr McCall had been discussing me for a few days as their school clerk, Iris, was leaving them for a job with more money. Would I like to replace her as clerk to the two schools? I told them I would have to ask my mother: she said yes.

I knew with all the certainly of my young innocent years that God was setting me on a new path. It was surely no coincidence that I had felt compelled to go home from Mrs Naden's and then going unexpectedly for fish and chips, especially to Whittington Moor; and then even being brave enough to go upstairs, which I wouldn't have dreamed of doing, which gave Mr Taylor and Mr McCall the opportunity of offering me the job. I knew that they would have contacted my mother, but thankfully what happened was the best way and was God's will for me. How could it be otherwise? I was certain that it was divine providence and I felt that my life had turned around.

The next morning I told Mrs Naden about the new job and she was pleased for me to have the opportunity, although she was sad I would be leaving. I promised that I would clean for her all day on Saturdays if she wanted me, which she did.

In the afternoon of my first day at my new job I had to go round to the kitchen and as I was unlocking the door with a Yale key it broke off in the lock! I was devastated, and not helped by a "friend" who was still at school, who said to me "You'll never be like Iris Charlesworth".

છ

I was very happy doing my job of keeping records and other clerical work, teaching backward children, taking money to the bank in Chesterfield, going to Stand Road baths at Whittington Moor to support the children, and helping the kitchen staff set the tables for lunch.

I was too shy to go into the staff room for morning coffee, although the teachers always invited me. I made myself a cup of cocoa by boiling water in a little pan on a gas ring in what we call the 'bottom room'. One morning I must have been distracted and George, a young boy, got hold of the pan handle, spilling some of the boiling water down his leg. I was devastated and frightened but took him to the teachers who dressed his leg and someone took him home. The next morning at the whole school assembly, Mr Taylor warned the children they must not to go into the 'bottom room' without permission.

Fearfully, I visited George but thankfully his parents told me it hadn't been my fault; he shouldn't have gone into that room as it was out of bounds. I was very grateful for their loving, understanding attitude, and also very thankful George that wasn't seriously hurt.

Privately, I arranged to attend Chesterfield Technical College three evenings a week, to learn shorthand and typing skills, also English.

જી

I hadn't been in the job for long when Gladys told me that our mother was going to marry Mr Marshall and that Marie and I were going to live at Dronfield with them. Crikey! I only knew him as the preacher who occasionally came to St Mary's Church to take the service. He wouldn't have Hugh: I didn't like that and it put me off this Mr Marshall. He was a lay reader in St John's Church and a retired headmaster and I didn't think he was behaving in a Christian way. Nonetheless, they married in St Mary's Church, Unstone Green. I had a new royal blue dress and sandals. Mr Marshall treated mother with respect.

The bungalow at Dronfield had three bedrooms and it was obvious that mother and Mr Marshall were going to sleep together. Marie and I were given the big bedroom next to the bathroom, which meant that the smaller bedroom in the middle could have been used by Hugh. He was working hard as an apprentice at Harrison's works in Unstone, which made scythes, sickles and edge tools, and he was attending Chesterfield College, learning to be a Master Grinder. I couldn't accept his being excluded but of course daren't say anything. What effect did that have on him?

Hugh had to stay with Gladys and her husband Billy and their young son David in the council house that they had been able to take over from our mother. Billy had served in the Eighth Army abroad and so he hadn't seen his son David until he was over three years old.

I vividly remember when David was born. Days before the baby was due I ran home every lunch time and after school, only to be disappointed, until one lunch time when he was born. Gladys, in bed in the front room, saw the top of my head bobbing over the low wall as I ran round the corner.

When David was a toddler Mother knitted him jerseys and short trousers in silk yarn with an animal border in a different colour. Gladys used to read out the stitches from the pattern. I was allowed to take David in his pram for short walks.

I comforted myself that Gladys would feed Hugh well and look after him, but I couldn't really understand mother agreeing to Hugh not being with us. He didn't say anything about it to me and I suppose he knew that I wasn't happy about having to live with my new step-father, leaving behind all that that was familiar to me. I was at an awkward age, when my body and emotions were changing. I couldn't call him Dad and so I didn't call him anything. It was easier for Marie, being only nine years old. She called him Daddy. I was quiet but respectful with him.

Our bungalow was full of light. It had three bedrooms, a large bathroom, long hall, front room and quite a large kitchen with a green mottled coal fire and a large oven at the side and a smaller oven over the top. The rooms had wooden floorboards, stained dark brown with carpets in the centre. The bathroom and kitchen had linoleum floor coverings. The bungalow was on the corner of Moorgate Crescent and so it had a very large garden with a lawn at the front and continued round following Moorgate Crescent at the rear leading down to a vegetable garden with fruit trees and a chicken run at the bottom with chickens

Thankfully, when I had calmed my emotions about Hugh being excluded, I was wise enough to think why shouldn't my mother have some happiness, after all she had been through in her life?

Mr Marshall, who had bought the bungalow and moved to Dronfield after his wife died, had two daughters and one son. They welcomed us into the family. Renee, the eldest, was married to Melvin and they were both very intelligent and serious. They had two daughters, Susan and Kathleen. Tom was married to Marcel – they were also very intelligent. They had one son, Tommy. Eileen was the youngest and she and her husband had six children, who were all lovely. We were able to visit them by bus to where they lived in different parts of Sheffield and they visited us. I especially liked Eileen. She was easy company and full of fun and I often went on my own to their home. She always had two tubs of washing soaking. We lost contact with Aunt Ethel and her family, and I had no idea why, but I never asked. It was sad, for I would have liked her to see mother in her new life. Also, I would have liked to keep in touch with Anthony and Marcia.

As a lay reader at St John's Church in Dronfield my stepfather expected me to attend there, so I divided my time between St John's and St Mary's. Through his position I was invited to join the prestigious Dronfield Park Avenue teenage set and went to their homes and out and about on different activities with them on Sunday afternoons.

Someone in my family has a photograph of mother and Mr Marshall at the children's home in Mickley Lane, Totley (now a Leonard Cheshire home). Mother, wearing a lovely dress and a trimmed straw hat, was presented with a bouquet. I knew she would have loved that.

☙

After we had moved in to Number 69, I took Marie to the 'first half' at the Dronfield Picture Palace. We were sitting downstairs and a young man I knew came in and sat next to me. When the film started he put his arm round my shoulders and brought his cheek up to mine. He was chewing gum! Marie was gazing up at us. I angrily asked him, "What do you think you are doing? You are being over-familiar. I am going to tell our Hugh." He quickly disengaged and left, never to sit next to me again. I suppose I was thought of as very 'prim and proper'. (The cinema closed down in 1964, to widespread disappointment. It was demolished some time later.)

☙

At that time Hill Top was just fields with a few farms and the chapel. Farther up Hallowes Lane from Moorgate Crescent there were beautiful big houses where business people lived, leading to the Hallowes Golf House and Club and the golf course and then the woods.

Chapter 2

When I was 16, Mr Ronald Biggin asked my stepfather if I would like to work in his family printing business in their Dronfield office. He had seen me in St John's Church. I went for an interview and was offered the job. It was a highly prestigious printing works: Mr Ronald was the office manager, his brother Mr Wilfred the works manager; their father Mr Arnold worked from his home at Aston Mount in Green Lane, and Mr Geoffrey, (Mr Ronald's son) was their travelling salesman.

Mr Taylor and Mr McCall understood this was an opportunity for me. I hadn't been using my secretarial skills with them and it was a small wage, but I had been happy working there.

So, I began at Arnold Biggin and Sons Ltd, 8am to 6pm Monday to Friday and Saturday mornings, and I would continue my evening classes to improve my skills. I had only been in the office for three weeks when I was summoned to the switchboard. It was big and I hadn't used it before, but what was even more daunting was the voice of Mr Ronald, the office manager. He was in the English Steel works office in Sheffield, where he went every afternoon as we did so much work for them. We knew that he had only one standard, '120 per cent'. He dictated a letter to me and I nearly died of fright! But when Mr Ronald returned he was so pleased with me he gave me ten shillings a week pay rise. That was a lot of money in 1949 and it gave a tremendous boost to my confidence.

Mr Geoffrey was handsome – I thought he was Clark Gable and Errol Flynn rolled into one! I don't think that he had any idea that I secretly admired him. Mr Geoffrey would visit canning factories in different parts of Norfolk and Lincolnshire and bring orders for the art department to create the canning labels. When he came back, I did secretarial work for him.

I proof read everything with Mr George Allen before it was printed. I also helped him prepare the weekly wages. The hours were long but the days flew. My secretarial skills were used daily. I loved to walk through the works, watching the machines working and sniffing the aromas of the inks and cleaning fluids. I'd briefly watch the artists in their upstairs room, creating their work where there was plenty of natural light from the big windows.

Mr Wilfred's two daughters, Cynthia and Valerie, came to the office and I have lovely memories of them both. Miss Cynthia always looked beautiful. My most vivid memories of her were when she wore a white hat and white gloves. One day Mr Geoffrey asked Miss Cynthia if she had been to a wedding: I thought this was very rude of him, but she just smiled serenely at him. Miss Valerie was more casual, like her father. I also vividly remember when Miss Cynthia was friendly with Mr John Ramsden, whom she later married. I still occasionally see them and Cynthia is still as beautiful and charming as she was then.

During the College break I worked on summer evenings at Mr Frank Hall's market gardens in Holmesdale, bunching and binding wallflowers. There were about twelve of us and we were in a big warehouse, filled with the glorious perfume of the flowers. Mr Geoffrey was courting Mr and Mrs Hall's eldest daughter, a petite, lovely, friendly young lady with fair curly hair. They later married.

Mr Hall was nicknamed 'Parsley' (I think it was only used behind his back), because he had grown parsley but for this season he supplied Sheffield market with the bunched wallflowers and with strawberries that we picked in the fields. One evening he asked me to go with him to his home, where his wife wanted me to do a job. He sat me at a table outside and asked me to hull two baskets of strawberries that the day staff had picked. He warned me he would look at my tongue to make sure I hadn't eaten any, so I did not dare to. In the event I was disappointed because he didn't look at my tongue, so I could have eaten one or two!

After he retired and sold up, he and his wife went to live in Jersey. The land and the surrounding area, now known as the Holmesdale estate, was sold for building houses and bungalows, shops and schools.

Also when I was 16 years old I joined the Dronfield Rangers. I hadn't been in the Girl Guides but the Rangers accepted me and we always enjoyed the evening meetings under the tuition of Miss Phyllis Buck, who we always knew as 'Phyl'. One week in the summer we holidayed in a caravan at the top of Dore Moor. It was wonderful. We hiked on the moors and took turns at cooking. Also, we went in pairs to dig a hole, after carefully measuring it out, and buried our portable toilet waste. I have often thought since then that there must be some good compost at the top of Dore Moor! On another occasion we went for a week in a caravan near Robin Hood's Bay.

ço

When I was 18 years old, I went with Phyl and the Rangers group for a week on the Isle of Arran in Scotland. We stayed in a boarding house, where the beds were set in the walls. It was a magical time for us, with the wonderful scenery, the sea and the beach, and the grass that was springy when we walked on it.

On the Monday evening we went to a hall for Scottish dancing and I met a gorgeous young man named George Macgregor. He had big dark brown eyes. He was training to be a tree surgeon. On the remaining evenings we all went walking as a group with George and his friends. We were only allowed to hold hands, no kissing.

For the Wednesday, Phyl organised a male guide to take us up Goat Fell, which is 2856 feet high. The climb was brilliant until a very thick cloud descended, obscuring everything and we found ourselves climbing up on loose slippery stones near the summit. It was very frightening and I was praying for God to help me – I have never known if my friends felt the same but I am sure they were. Happily, we reached the summit without harm. I realized afterwards that if we had been in real danger the tour guide would have turned back and I knew that Phyl wouldn't let us go into any danger.

Reaching the summit was an achievement and built my confidence. Going down again was really more dangerous than going up, but I did it without giving fear a thought and I have never forgotten this.

I was heartbroken that George wasn't there to say goodbye on the Saturday morning as we waited for the ferry. The other young men also were missing and for a while later I pined for George. We laughed afterwards about it – these young men would befriend any young women who visited the island.

Phyl worked for Lady Bower Reservoir power station and one Saturday afternoon she organised for our group and the Chesterfield Rovers to go under the reservoir. It was a frightening to think of all that water over my head but with the young men going first, we climbed up a short ladder attached to the wall and then onto a small mesh platform that continued until we reached the route to the exit. I remember standing and looking at the reservoir and thinking, "Wow! I've actually been underneath that!"

On Sundays we often went hiking with the Chesterfield Rovers and a group from Barnsley. One day the snow was so deep on the Pennines that we were pushing through snow up to the top of our legs. We had the time of our lives!

I became friendly with Frank, one of the Rovers, who was tall and had a look of the film star Randolph Scott. We used to walk in the moonlight near the

Dronfield Hallowes golf course. Being so innocent we never kissed. I have very often regretted that I stopped seeing him on his own. One of his friends told me that Frank had made a big cardboard heart, painted it red before tearing it in half! Frank became a teacher and later was a head teacher.

We had sound, 'healthy in body and mind', times in the Rangers. Phyl must have worked very hard on our behalf. I often think of her and I know that she is safe with Jesus. She cannot hear, but I salute a wonderful, loving yet strict and wise lady and I thank her for the valuable lessons I learned through her. I am pleased to have had those years preparing me for the challenges that lay ahead for me.

On Sunday evenings, after attending the evening service at St John's, I loved to listen to the half-hour radio programme with Paul West and his band and Paul's wife, Jo Stafford, singing.

I was used to walking up the dark Hallowes Lane, lit by gas lamps, on the way home. One evening I was near the end of the back lane when I spotted a tall man with his trilby pulled down, staring at me. I was uneasy and looked back down the lane as best I could through the darkness and saw a lady walking up. It was Della and I turned back to join her, saying that I had been startled by this tall man with glaring eyes, who was looking at me. "Come on, Hazel," she said, "you are safe with me."

The figure was still standing there, but as we approached, Della exclaimed, "Oh, it's my husband." We laughed, because he was a most gentle unassuming man ever. He had been waiting there because he wasn't sure whether Della was coming on the back lane or up the hill! Seeing me he thought it was Della but didn't recognize my coat. Thankfully, they had a sense of humour but whenever I met them in the daylight, I always blushed. I never dreamed buses would come up Hallowes Lane but services began in 1956, although having asked for them the local house owners didn't want bus stops outside their home.

Chapter 3

I was happy at Arnold Biggins for eight years, but Mr Allen retired through ill-health and the office system changed with new staff. I decided to 'spread my wings'. I left on the Friday without a job but planned to look around for another post.

On the Monday morning I went to the Chesterfield Job Centre who pointed me to Standall Tools Ltd in Mickley Lane, Dronfield Woodhouse, where they made mining tools. It was owned by two brothers who were looking for a secretary. I was told that there a bus went from Wreakes Lane in Dronfield to Holmesfield, and the times and directions from the bus stop – past the pub, down a slope, turn left and the works was a few yards on. I caught the bus back from Chesterfield and then a Holmesfield bus, which was always a double-decker

Mr George Hall was the office manager and Mr Joseph was the works manager. Mr George offered me the job as secretary for himself and for Mr Stokes, the travelling salesman. He told me they had considered several applicants but that I could start immediately if I wanted to. His former secretary was ill and wasn't returning to work.

Mr George took me into a large general office and introduced me to Rae, who worked part-time preparing the wages and invoices, and to Carole who did general office work. He then showed me the canteen where I was provided with a pot of tea and sandwiches.

I felt I would be happy there and was keen to start immediately, but I had arranged to take my mother that afternoon to see Grace Kelly in the film 'The Swan' at the Chesterfield Odeon. So Mr George let me ring Mrs Hallas in the bungalow next to ours to let my mother know and that I would take her on Saturday afternoon instead. I waited whilst Mrs Hallas called to mother through the hedge: she was delighted that I had found a job on my first day out of work. I later met Mr Stokes and had also a good working relationship with him.

I enjoyed the new job but often remembered my old boss, Mr Allen. When he retired he and his wife and their daughter, Christine, went to live in Blackpool. Sadly they had only been there for three months when Mr Allen was knocked over by a big dog and suffered a broken hip. Complications led to pneumonia and he died. I was heartbroken. I had the greatest respect and fondness for him and felt that after working all his life he should have been able to enjoy some years of happy retirement. It took me quite a while to accept.

❧

I often saw a man with blonde wavy hair watching me through a window but I ignored him. Walking home one Friday evening on the back lane, I met Alfie, one of the workmen. He had been waiting for me; I was over an hour late finishing work that day. He told me that he had waited because the man with blonde hair, Roy Helliwell, wanted to take me to the Dronfield pictures that evening. I said "No, certainly not." Alfie said he had waited all this time to ask me because Roy was too nervous to ask himself. So, feeling sorry for Alfie, who had waited all that time, I met Roy outside the picture house. It definitely wasn't love at first sight, but he was very kind and clean. He was 11 years older than me and had a motorbike. I couldn't get rid of him.

He lived with his mother, Lily, who was very possessive of him. Their home was a stone cottage owned by Mrs Belk, mother-in-law to Joe, who was Roy's elder brother. They had moved there from Millhouses in Sheffield, when the cottage became empty through a death. It was very small, with a kitchen living room. It had a coal fire with side ovens just as mother had had. There was also a small room leading to stairs up to two bedrooms. There was no hot water and an outside toilet. I used to go there from work and Lily always had a good meal ready. Then I knitted and watched television. There wasn't much else to do and so I would ask Roy to take me home early so I could clean my shoes, wash my hair, bath and get to bed.

Lily told me about Roy's dad who had worked on a furnace. He had been a quiet man who loved to go to his allotment where he would grow his vegetables. We have one of his ferns in our front garden, transplanted from Millhouses then from Dronfield Woodhouse.

Roy was often tinkering about with his motorbike and he liked to repair clocks. When we watched the television I had to bite my lip so as not to laugh at his mother, who would say of every man she saw on the screen, "Our Roy could do better than him; our Roy could do better than him." Roy played the mouth organ and when Larry Adler came on – oh dear! I often wanted to ask "Why doesn't he, then?", but I kept silent and let it go over my head.

On Sundays we had a ride out on Roy's motorbike and very often we joined Les on his motorbike with his wife Phyllis in the sidecar. We would go to Kedleston Hall where the men would fish whilst Phyllis and I walked or chatted while we sat knitting.

I thought I was getting on well with Lily, but one evening when Joan, Roy's niece, said something – I can't remember what it was – Lily said to her, "It's a shame she left the Biggins." Joan protested, "You can't say things like that." But she had meant it and it wasn't the first time she had said it. The first time I thought, 'Right, that told me, you want to keep Roy to yourself.' I was his first girlfriend and I suppose she couldn't understand me. I was quiet, I didn't drink alcohol I liked to knit and sew. Most important, I was a believing Christian.

I didn't let him have sex before we married. He didn't attract me enough also I was fearful. I wasn't sure that I wanted to marry him and I knew I wanted my husband to be the first. I thought that I might fall in love with someone else.

However, I eventually agreed to marry him. I was 26 and wanted children and I thought we would have a good marriage. Roy was kind and had a very nice personality but I knew I would have to get him away from Lily. There was an incident quite early on that shocked me. I was not used to wearing jewellery and was also quite frugal, so I chose an inexpensive engagement ring, naïvely thinking that Roy would be saving for our own home. I was speechless when I learned that Lily had forced him to buy one for her!

ॐ

I provided for my family to prepare the home catering for my wedding. The baking was done by Gladys and her close friend Daisy Monk, who lived three doors up from Gladys at Unstone Green; I had known her and her mother all my life. I bought the wedding cake and bridesmaid's dresses for Joan, Roy's niece, my niece Enid, Albert and Bessie's daughter and Janet, one of Eileen's daughters; and the accessories, their presents, and the bouquets.

The money was not easy to find. I was supporting my mother with money and buying my cigarettes – silly fool that I was for starting to smoke when I was 22 years old. I dressed quietly but smartly, in keeping with being a secretary, and I knitted myself twin sets and jumpers. So, I had almost spent up, but I borrowed the beautiful dress and veil that Marie used for her wedding in the previous year.

We married on 21 March 1959, the first day of spring. Billy gave me away and Joe was Roy's best man. After the ceremony at St John's church, Lily stood outside and shouted "This is the church that has stolen my son", before heading off to the Green Dragon pub opposite the church. Dora followed her, which made me feel safe, for Dora would restrain her if she tried to spoil my wedding reception. My family and friends would have been very angry with her, some members of my family weren't happy about me marrying Roy. I had placed Lily between Dora and Joan at the table. Roy and I had arranged for the wedding reception to be in the Church Hall. I have never forgotten Mr Kyme, the schoolteacher who took the photographs, climbing on to a cupboard so he could get all of us in the picture as we sat at the tables.

We spent our honeymoon, Sunday to Saturday, in a small boarding house in Blackpool that had been recommended to me. I had told Roy that I wanted to wait until we were there so that our first time as husband and wife could be special. I could not have comfortably given myself to Roy with Lily being in such close proximity in the next bedroom at home. I suppose I did not trust Lily not to pull a fast one and be "ill" to prevent us going. She was very quiet on the Sunday morning but I think she must have realized that if she tried to prevent our going, Dora and my family would have stood up for us.

Dora came to take us to Sheffield railway station. Before setting off, Roy got out of the car and hurried back into the cottage; I had a few minutes of anxiety but he came back and we set off. I was filled with hope. There was just one other newly married young couple in the boarding house. The husband was a talented pianist.

Roy telephoned Dora twice a day to make sure his mother was all right. Each time I held my breath. What would I do if Lily claimed to be ill and we had to return?

Fortunately, the eventuality didn't occur. Dora wouldn't have spoiled our holiday and she was wise to her mother's tricks.

We lived with his mother. Not good, definitely not good, but in my naivety I thought it would only be a temporary arrangement.

や

In September I was expecting a baby. I vividly remember Lily's attitude when Roy and I told her. She was angry, saying "You haven't been married five minutes." In fact it had been from March to September, and I made that six months. I was 26 years old and Roy was 37. I was upset, bewildered and shocked. Had she expected us not to have children? Was she jealous? She flounced upstairs. I looked at Roy and he said, "She's bound to say that". I felt betrayed; why was she 'bound to say it'? Roy had agreed that we would to try to make a baby in September, but I had a sinking feeling that this baby wasn't wanted. However, good sense took control. and already I felt a fierce protective love for it. Lily had told me previously that she had had several miscarriages and had been a 'wet nurse' with having so much milk.

My routine continued. I was strong and had very little morning sickness. I bought white and lemon three-ply baby wool and began to knit in preparation. I bought white wool for my mother who wanted to knit a big shawl.

や

Hugh met Barbara at Tyzack's, Sheffield, where he now worked, and I loved her from the moment I saw her. She was perfect for him, outgoing and confident, and she and her family had been brought up in a loving united family. I felt sure that Hugh would be right for Barbara, although he could be difficult and was very shy. They married on 10 October 1959, I was one month pregnant. It was obvious to everyone they were deeply in love. It was a lovely wedding and reception.

Hugh had bought a stone-built cottage at the bottom of Hallowes Lane and he and Barbara moved in after their wedding. I was so pleased that Hugh had Barbara and they seemed to be a blessed couple. At school Hugh had been clever enough to go on to university but in those days it was not possible. They had a little dog and went walking in the country. Hugh had a Zephyr car.

৯

I worked for seven months so as to get my full insurance payment. Indeed, I was still working when I was eight months' pregnant but Mr George Hall eventually found a lady to take over from me. He asked me to stay to show her the ropes. By this time I was almost nine months' pregnant and although I was very strong, I had to say to Mr George, "I need to leave or I'll be having the baby here!" He laughed and told me they had a big wheelbarrow! He advised me to get a home of our own, away from Roy's mother. He gave me five pounds for nappies.

I always give credit where it is due and every lunch time after Roy and I were married, Lily sent me a basin of hot food to eat in the canteen. But I also knew that she wanted to keep me out of the way! She was a good cook even though she only had the oven at the side of the coal fire and a gas ring.

Lily wanted me to give birth in the cottage but Sister Guyler put her foot down. There was no bathroom, no hot water, the toilet was outside and the cottage was damp and dark. It was no place to give birth and I wouldn't have had agreed to do so. So, on Sunday evening Dora took me to my mother's for the birth. She had put a single bed in the front room and before getting into bed I had a long soak in the bath. I then slept, waking up just after 1am with pains. It was Monday 13 June and a most beautiful summer day. Sister Guyler came but I was in labour for hours, walking round the room. In the afternoon Sister Guyler said if I hadn't had the baby by 4pm I would have to go into hospital.

Roy called in and then went to work; he wasn't a shirker. Sister Guyler came back and examined me, declaring "Not long now" before lying down on the bed herself! Roy came back and was soon pacing the long hall.

Stephen came quickly, with his left arm on his head, so his hand was born first. He had a fine sprinkling of fair hair and he was beautiful. His eyes and lips were closed and he had a clean pink and white complexion.

Naturally I was tired. Dora brought Lily, who looked at the baby and said, "Oh, isn't he like our Roy". Tired as I was, I thought, 'Who does she think he would look like, Frank the butcher?'

Three weeks after giving birth to Stephen, I made an appointment with the vicar of St John the Baptist in Dronfield for prayers as a new mother to be cleansed; it was called being 'churched'. As I knelt at the altar and the vicar prayed with me I felt renewed again with the Holy Spirit and strengthened. I have never forgotten that time.

A week later I very reluctantly went back to the cottage. It was always "Our Roy's baby" and "Have you seen our Roy's baby?" I didn't react, only in my thoughts.

Before Stephen was born Lily told me I had to wash his clothes in his bath water. I was certainly not going to do that, after all those years of my mother's immaculate washing, starching and ironing and how she had washed our clothes after Stephen's birth. Lily had all her and Roy's clothes, towels, bedding and everything else washed and ironed by the Snowite laundry in Millhouses, who collected every week. I bought a small washing machine that heated the water and on this occasion Roy knew better than to oppose me, especially since it was bought with my money.

Lily resented me being in her house and resented Roy giving me housekeeping money. She had told me firmly that she wasn't giving me any money and also that I had to do the cooking. She liked to drink alcohol, so it wasn't a happy time for me. I became so thin that my dresses hung around my ankles.

Stephen was a wonderfully contented baby, he slept all the time and didn't cry. I took him out in his pram as much as possible and thankfully he didn't pick up the atmosphere in the house.

When I had first known Roy, he gave his mother his unopened wage envelope on Fridays. I was horrified that she didn't even say 'Thank you'. I couldn't hold my tongue and told them, so she began to thank him. However, when I finished work he would not give me his wage envelope, just £3. It was not easy because I knew that Roy's money was going on alcohol and on Lily's taste for new clothes. She would often go into Sheffield to buy a new dress that she would wear only a few times before tearing it up for rags. I was horrified but said nothing; I had been brought up not to waste anything. Roy must have continued to give her money and I couldn't buy enough food to cook for us from the £3, as Lily had provided and we had always ate well. I give her this, but then she had plenty of money.

One day as I was buying food in Mr and Mrs Clayton's post office and grocery shop, which was only a few yards away. I saw the shelves moving and the next thing I knew was Mr Clayton helping me walk back home. I had fainted. Two days later Lily, who always ate in her armchair in front of the fireplace, questioned me when I had given her a cooked lunch, "Where is the meat?" I was carrying Roy's plate of food to the table and the room began swimming round and everywhere was going black. I remember shouting something – no idea what – and I dropped the plate of food. I woke up to find myself on the settee. Lily and Roy looked concerned.

Lily told me that she would do the cooking again. I think Mr and Mrs Clayton and the neighbours had told her and Roy how ill I was looking. After fainting in their shop When Mr Clayton took me back he had said to Lily, "This young lady needs looking after". With Lily cooking once more I had time to take Stephen out and about, so Lily had the house to herself. When I took Stephen to the baby clinic a nurse arranged for the doctor to prescribe iron tablets for me.

Roy sided with Lily and he always appeared to be happy. I knew I had made a big mistake marrying him, but in faith and hope I kept thinking life would improve. I had stopped going to church because Roy was so opposed to it, but Stephen was baptized in September at St John's Church and afterwards we had tea at my mother's. Dora and her husband Colin and my nephew David (Gladys and Billy's eldest son) were his godparents.

৯

One morning in the doctor's clinic I met a young lady who told me she also lived in Dronfield Woodhouse. Her name was Rita and she was expecting her first baby. We became friends. One day I was taking Stephen for a walk to Bradway to buy wool to knit for him, and she came to the cottage to see me. Lily told me I had to stop her coming because she was only after Stephen's nappies! I found that very hurtful. I went to see Rita after she had given birth to her little girl. Their home was luxurious and there were piles of gorgeous baby clothes around.

Her husband was charming and as I was leaving, he said to Rita, "Darling, you go and soak in the bath, then paint your toe nails". Rita took pride in her feet. I could see they were genuinely in love and I felt a pain at my own life, which seemed so different. I wasn't jealous of their lovely home or the baby presents – material things as such didn't matter to me – it was the obvious closeness of this husband and wife that made me feel empty. Unfortunately, I lost Rita's friendship sometime later when her husband's work was transferred and they moved away.

Chapter 4

On Stephen's first Christmas day, Lily cooked the lunch and Roy's sister Dora, Colin her husband, Joan and her new boyfriend Bernard came to join us. I loved Dora and her daughter Joan. They were both highly intelligent and Joan was so clever she went to a private school. She also had elocution lessons. They and Colin loved dogs and horses and Joan rode in gymkhanas. Dora was sympathetic to my plight at home and rebuked her mother when she was nasty with me, as did Joan, but to no avail.

We were sitting round the small table, ready to enjoy the meal, when Lily suddenly threw her plate of food at me. We were in shock as she stormed off upstairs with Roy and Dora following and we heard her shouting, "Make her go, I don't want her here". It was so embarrassing for all of us: Joan had only recently become friendly with Bernard but they later married and had two gorgeous sons. Colin was angry; he had no time for Lily. What was most hurtful for me was to hear Roy telling his mother that although I was his wife, he would look after her. Dora took her back with them and Roy followed on his motorbike. He was gone so long I thought he and Lily must be staying at Dora's house. When he returned he said Lily would be staying with Dora for a few days.

After almost two weeks and with him going to see his mother every evening and on Saturday afternoons and Sunday, he came back on a Wednesday evening and said Lily was returning the next day. I couldn't bear it, my nerves were so shattered. I was up all that night and packed everything that belonged to Stephen and me on Stephen's pram and early on Thursday morning Roy watched me set off to live with my mother. He made not a word of protest and the hurt and rejection went deep within me: he seemed to be relieved I was going! When does hope die?

My mother wasn't expecting me (they still hadn't a telephone), but she was worried about me and so I joined her, my sister Marie, her husband Raymond and their young son Shaun at the house. Marie and Raymond went to work. Roy came to see me most evenings and Saturday and Sunday afternoons to see Stephen, as he was asleep when Roy came in the evenings.

One evening Roy told me he wanted me to go to the dark back lane nearby with him to have sex. I was so insulted and angry. It was a public walk. What did he think I was, a prostitute? Where was the respect? Did I and his baby mean so little to him? For him to stay with his mother whilst Stephen and I were lodgers in my mother's home?

His proposal was deeply offensive and it infuriated me. It was an insult to our marriage and to me as a woman, reducing the marriage that had begun for me with such hope, to a purely carnal level. I hid my anger and told him to go if that was all he was coming for. As he left, something in me died: my expectation of a good marriage and having a home together, growing closer as a family with more babies and Roy coming to know Jesus.

I daren't tell my mother and Marie what he had said; my brothers would have thrashed him. I wouldn't have allowed him to come back but I was homeless and I couldn't work, having to care for Stephen. Mother looked after one–year-old Shaun. Out of the £3 that Roy gave me each week I had to pay my mother for living at her house and I had to buy the essentials for Stephen. There was no family allowance in those days.

I had reduced my smoking to a couple a day when I knew I was pregnant, knowing that I was a silly fool for smoking at all. Phyl, our Ranger captain, had taught us about keeping our bodies and minds healthy. At least when Stephen was born he was a beautiful pink and white and he retained his lovely complexion.

I couldn't possibly go back to Lily's, she hated me. There was no space for Stephen and me in her small bungalow where we could be away from her. There was no going back there and I knew now that Roy's promises in his wedding vows had been meaningless. I thought 'I should have stayed at Biggin's', just as Lily had previously said on at least four occasions.

I needed new brassieres after Stephen was born and hadn't the money, so had to pay weekly for them. I had knitted a lot of baby clothes and had made Stephen's long white night gowns before he was born. I had bought white three-ply wool for my mother, who offered to knit a beautiful big shawl; it must have taken some knitting and patience. Of course I didn't know if my baby would be a boy or girl, but I bought the big pram, cot, bath and the necessities that a new baby needed from my saved wages and maternity money.

୨୦

Gladys called to tell me that the people who lived in Miss Barber's flat at Hounscliffe, Unstone Green, had left and that we should go and look at the property. Gladys stayed on the footpath opposite the entrance drive. Miss Barber was pleased to see Stephen and me but when I asked about the flat (I had no idea how much rent it would be) she told me that a family was moving in the following week. Then, very shyly and blushing, she told me she was cooking for a friend who was coming for supper. As I went back to Gladys, I shook my head and said "No". She cried.

I can still see Gladys in my memory, leaning on the wall, watching me cry as I wheeled Stephen back to Hallowes Lane. I was told later that Miss Barber was friendly with Captain Moore whom she later married. So that was who she was cooking for. I can also still see Miss Barber's beautiful face, excited at the prospect of her guest coming. I thank God for that memory, one amongst many wonderful recollections of how Miss Barber helped us as children.

However, in March my sister Hilda came and told me of a cottage for sale in Snape Hill Lane just above the Cooperative store; it was £300. She took me to see it. Excited, I couldn't wait for Roy to come that Saturday afternoon but when I told him he said he couldn't take it on. He had a good job so I knew that his refusal was because he didn't want to leave his mother. I was so angry at his response that I fought him with my fists, fighting for our future and Stephen's. I was desperate. Where was God in all this mess? I had begun to think he had deserted me and I had difficulties remembering his promises in his word and how good he had been to me in my life. But no, he hadn't deserted me: Roy admitted he hadn't any money saved.

I asked him to seek help from Mr George Hall. As Roy's employer he knew we would be able to pay him back. Roy refused. I didn't think it right that I should go to Mr George but nonetheless I suggested this to Roy. I know that it must have cost Roy's nerves dearly, but he did ask Mr George who, as a business man, said that he wanted present security. But Roy had nothing, no bank account, nothing saved, zero.

In the end we had to borrow the money privately. Who would believe that Roy had worked from the age of 14 and yet had nothing to his name but a push bike and a motorbike. He smoked heavily and he hadn't spent on me, but he had no money at age 39.

I had overheard a female who lived near Roy and Lily saying that there was always something missing in people who were born of an old father. I let that go – she hadn't named me but we knew it was me she was getting at. I had always been a home-bird and Hugh was quiet but Marie, who was five years younger, was a lively soul, as were Jack, Albert and Hilda.

஧

We bought the little house. On the Sunday afternoon before we moved in and, knowing that we were now secure in having a home, I took Stephen in his pram to Lily's. All the way there I was expecting Roy to meet us but he did not. When we arrived at the cottage he was sitting with his mother watching the television. Lily and the neighbours were thrilled to see Stephen. Lily had a good meal cooked for me. When I went back home to my mother's house, again on my own, my mother was surprised. She thought I might have stayed with them, but I would not, no way.

On the afternoon that I wheeled Stephen in his pram from my mother's to move in, I felt a peace go through me as I reached the corner of the Cooperative Stores: we were going home. The next morning I woke next to Roy to hear Stephen gurgling happily in his cot in the next small bedroom. I went in and he was waving his arms and kicking his legs – he was happy too.

Our cottage in Snape Hill Lane was second up from the bottom in a row of six. We had a small garden at the back, two bedrooms, cellar, kitchen and front room with a door leading into a small patch before the footpath. The house was full of light. We were very happy with the neighbours. The cottage next to ours changed hands several times as young married couples came and then bought larger homes. I missed them but would still see them as we are out and about.

Once we had moved into Snape Hill Lane I made sure I held the purse strings. I gave Roy money for his football coupon and petrol and I bought his cigarettes for him .

✇

While Hugh was still working at Tyzack's, he got together with some friends who were expert builders and together they built a bungalow on the back garden of their cottage. It had three bedrooms, a bathroom, a long hall, kitchen and a very large lounge Their daughter Lynne was born on 13 August 1961.

I had the feeling that Hugh never liked Roy. I once heard Hugh telling him that he was looking after Barbara – Hugh's wife, but his words just went over Roy's head.

Roy spent almost all of his spare time with Lily. I never knew what time he was coming home and nine times out of ten the meal I had cooked for him was dried up: he had eaten with Lily. He also called to see her before going to work and took his sandwiches to have his lunch with her. I gave up cooking for him and fed just Stephen and myself. At least we had our little home.

Stephen loved jellies and would sit in his high chair, banging his spoon on the little table saying, "More, more, more". He began to talk properly at ten months. He had an inquiring mind. The young lady we had bought the house from had left a gate separating the living room from the kitchen and Stephen somehow managed to squeeze through the bars. One morning he was sitting on the kitchen floor shaking a drum of Vim powder from the sink cupboard all round him. Roy made it more secure. It was a Friday afternoon, when

Stephen was 11 months that he began to walk: he was sitting on the living room carpet and I saw him just get up and walk!

Another memory that I recall, amongst all the others, is when he was two years old and we were in Chesterfield. We met my sister Gladys in front of the Gas showroom window. Talking with Gladys we were amazed to see Stephen inside the window. The shop was advertising something with a chicken going up and down bending to the floor and he had gone into the window display to see how it worked.

တ

Roy managed to stop smoking and so did I when Stephen was two years old. I constantly praised him for that and bought him glacier mints to suck. It must have been very hard for him after being a heavy smoker since his teen years, but his cough lessened and he felt better in himself. It was easier for me because I had only smoked two a day and I took Stephen in his push chair up Hill Top and did deep breathing. En route, we called each week at Steel's hardware shop on Dronfield main road and I bought Stephen a matchbox toy.

We had a coal-coke fire and while we were out Stephen and I collected kindling and pieces of sticks to burn. Our coal was delivered down the hole at the front of the house, directly into the cellar. The Cooperative store at that time had three sections: food and where we could buy milk tokens et cetera, the middle was a butcher's, and at the end nearest Snape Hill Lane there was a draper's shop. I loved to go into the drapers where they would put wool assignments for me to buy when I could afford to. In those days we were paid dividend money.

သ

Despite Roy spending so much time with Lily, early one Sunday morning we woke to rattling on our bedroom window. It was Lily throwing pebbles against the glass. I don't know how she got there from Dronfield Woodhouse before 5am. Roy let her in and I made a pot of tea. She told me several times to go back to bed but I said no, thinking this was my home and she wasn't going to take over. Eventually Roy took her home in the Isetti, his little bubble car. He had bought the car from one of his work colleagues and could drive it on his motorbike licence. He didn't return until late that evening.

From this event and others, I began to realize the power that Lily had over Roy. He wasn't the strongest of men and hadn't been in the forces or away from home. At school his older brother had shielded him from bullies but even so he couldn't cope and was moved to a private school. He was full of insecurities and often seemed mentally unbalanced. Lily must have been frightening him emotionally as to what she would do if he deserted her and he wasn't strong enough to withstand her. Joe, Roy's elder brother, was a strong character and I once heard him tell Lily that he was looking after his wife Renee and she hadn't to interfere. She didn't nor did she dare to, since she lived in her mother's cottage. Mrs Belk lived across the drive and Renee's sister, Rae, who worked in Standall's general office, lived next door to Lily.

Dora used to take Lily, Roy, Stephen and me to Bridlington for the day. Stephen loved the beach and made sand pies. We took sandwiches and flasks. Travelling there and back, Lily or Roy talked incessantly and I used to switch off from their twittering. Sometimes they both talked at the same time. It was a good job that I was quiet. I was very thin and must have been only a size 8. Joan, who was so slender, gave me some lovely clothes that fitted me. There was one particular dress that I loved, a sleeveless brown and white check, and I wore it constantly.

Marie and Raymond's daughter Karen was born on 17 December 1963. Hugh and Barbara's son, Andrew, was born in 11 January 1964 and the family moved into their newly built bungalow in 1968. The old cottage was demolished to make a driveway leading up to the garage that Hugh had built, and the stones were used for walling and for sale.

In the years before Stephen started school, he and I spent a lot of time in Cliffe Park, Dronfield. I always got a lot of knitting done whilst Stephen played with the other young children in the sand pit.

Over the years Hill Top and the Hallowes estate has been built up and the Gosforth Valley housing development site was created in 1967. There were new schools, including the Gosforth School for 11-14 year-olds, which was opened in 1954.

Holmesdale Infants School on The Avenue was opened in 1957 and Stephen began there in 1965. Mrs Millington was the headmistress. Stonelow Junior School for 7-11 year-olds opened in 1967 and Stephen was one of the first pupils. Mr Harry was the headmaster and Mr Hodgson was his deputy.

Gladys Buxton School, which had opened in 1959 on Oakhill Road, with Mr Eyre as head master, was Stephen's next school, taking him up to 14 years of age, after which he went to Henry Fanshawe School in Green Lane.

Gladys Buxton school pupils merged with Gosforth School in 1990 before the pupils attended Henry Fanshawe School. Then Henry Fanshawe School accommodated all the pupils from 11 years up when Gosforth School closed and later was demolished in 2005 for houses and a new medical centre, dental surgery and a chemist shop were built on the site. Gladys Buxton School, now called The Gladys Buxton Centre, serves different activities in the community.

I used to wait at the Infants School with a few other mothers to take our children home for lunch. A group of us were also there when they finished at 3pm and several of us went down to Dronfield Cliffe Park where the children could run about and play. I took Stephen's three-wheel bike and he loved to gather a pile of leaves on the top path and then ride his bike through them, repeating it several times. Stephen and I almost lived in Cliffe park on Saturdays and in the school holidays. He loved playing in the sand pit with the other children. I got plenty of knitting done! He also had very happy

times with the Bradwell family who lived near us at the
bottom of Cecil Road

One morning, when he was 6 years old, Stephen
didn't want to go to school. He told me that he would
help me with my housework. He must have been
working up to this and I thought something or someone
must have upset him. I felt protective towards him, but I
told him he had to go to school to learn. He never said
again that he didn't want to go, which I thought was a
success for both of us.

Stephen joined the 4th Dronfield Cubs at St Paul's
church and greatly enjoyed his Friday evenings and all
the activities.

ೂ

We eventually paid off the loan and I then began
saving every penny and investing. In the years between
Stephen's fourth and eleventh years, we went to
Saturday jumble sales. We queued for an hour or so with
friends who we came to know. We all enjoyed it. I was
mad on teapots then and over the years I built up a
lovely collection that I displayed. Those Saturdays and
the people we came to know were precious and I
cherished how Stephen stood with me with such
patience.

Stephen started at Stonelow Junior School when he
was seven years old and was one of the first pupils at
this new school. He stayed there for lunch and I missed
him very much in the first few weeks. I used to walk
past the school at lunch time to make sure he was all

Me, dressed in a lovely jumper knitted by my mother

Probably my first photograph

Me, looking my young best for the camera. I was so proud of that ribbon and bow in my hair.

Me, outside our house at 227 Sheffield Road, Unstone Green

Above: My sister Marie, the youngest in our family

Left: My brother Hugh, who was two years older than me

St. Mary's Church, Unstone Green, on a Sunday School outing. Mrs Naden at far left with white glove; Miss Barber at top right with straw hat; Captain Mitchell is standing, far right.

Above: The Chesterfield Rovers and Dronfield Rangers. Hazel in white, front row; Frank is top right

Left: Mr Marshall, my stepfather, with my mother and Marie

Below: Marie, 18, and me, 23, on holiday in Scarborough

Above: My great-grandfather

Above: Hugh, pictured outside our mother's bungalow at No 69 Hallowes Lane

Left: Me, age 24, with earrings. They were a present from Marie

Above: My brother Hugh, pictured on holiday by the lake in Peasholm Park, Scarborough

Hugh and Marie on a day trip to Skegness

Hugh on holiday

Hugh (left) pictured with a friend during his National Service

Above Left: Marlene Undrell and me at the Dronfield Rangers' caravan at Dore Moor

Above: Me with Marie at No 69 Hallowes Lane

Left: L-R, Marie, Enid, Me, Jack, my mother and Patricia

Below: L-R, Gladys, her son Christopher, and me at No 69 Hallowes Lane

The wedding of Raymond and Marie, 15 March 1958.
L-R: Pauline, Raymond, Ken, Patricia, Marie and me

My wedding day, 21 March 1959. Some names, from left, Barbara and
Hugh, Jack (kneeling) with his son Michael, the boys are nephews Rodney,
Paul, Philip, behind them are Renee, Dora, Hilda, my Mother holds
Patricia; the boys at front right are my nephews

My wedding : L-R, Joe, Enid, Mother, Roy, me, Joan, Janet, Lily, Billy

The traditional wedding pictures: the happy couple at the church and my very fine three-tiered wedding cake

*Our wedding day,
21 March 1959:
L-R, Marie with Shaun,
Roy, Joan and in front, my
step-sister Eileen holds up
her youngest daughter for
me to kiss*

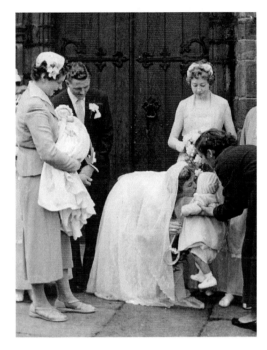

*On our honeymoon and
Roy and I step out on
Blackpool's famous
promenade*

Hugh and Barbara's Wedding, 10 October 1959. L-R, Jack, Margaret, Mother, Hugh, Barbara, Carol, Mary, Janet, John, Patricia

Hugh and Barbara's Wedding
L-R, Brenda, Marie, Hugh and Marie's husband Raymond

Pictured at No 69 Hallowes Road: L-R, Raymond, Marie with Shaun,
Mother and me. 'Prince' is in the background

Above: my brother Jack

Left: my brother Albert

*Left: Jack and his wife
Violet on their wedding day*

*Below: Jack with his
daughter, Patricia*

*Jack and
Patricia at the
seaside*

Stephen and Chris at Butlins, Skegness

Roy with Stephen, after voting at Holmesdale School

Stephen and friends make tea at the Spitewinter Youth Camp

At Hallowes Golf: L-R, Kay, Marie, Karen, Stephen and 'Prince', the dog

Yarmouth, August 1980, a holiday taken reluctantly after Stephen's broken engagement; L-R, Ray, Karen, Roy, Marie, Arthur, Me, Sue, Betty

Also taken on that holiday, L-R, Sue, Gladys, Ray, Marie, Roy, me

Stephen, age 20, before his illness

Stephen, after his illness, pictured on a walk at Ashover

right. They didn't finish until 3.30pm, when I would meet him and we would go into the park or for a walk through the wood.

I have never forgotten Stephen's face when he was eight years old and with some birthday money he bought me a long lemon-coloured plastic box for me to keep my knitting needles from the Cooperative drapers shop. He had thought it out for himself and it was a lovely surprise. I still have the box and still treasure it. I adored him from the day he was born and I still do.

Stephen became very friendly with Chris Hall who lived on Marsh Avenue. He almost lived with them and often went with them to Butlins holiday camp for a week. I was always happy he was with a lovely family. Pat had another boy Dean, who Stephen adored and carried him on his shoulders. I learned that Pat's mum had taken over my job at Unstone schools when I left at 16 years of age and I thought that was quite a coincidence.

Stephen had just started at Gladys Buxton secondary school when I was hanging out the washing and a neighbour, Mrs Gambles who lived in the first villa house above our row and with whom I was friendly, called over the wall to tell me that a house had gone up for sale in the next road, Alexandra Road. We could see it from our house, as the three cottages between us had been knocked down, having been condemned because they hadn't a cellar. Stephen and the kids played on this bit of waste land. We had shared a toilet with the bottom house so now we were able to have one each. Our neighbours at the top had their own outside toilet. Joan and Norman at the fourth cottage up had no children and had their small bedroom made into a bathroom.

I went across to look at the house. Mr Gregory, who had lived there for over 40 years, had died. I knew we could get a 90 per cent grant to have a bathroom built. I had not previously considered moving again, but it must have been God's will for us. It was priced at £8,000 and I was confident we could get that price for our own little house.

Again, excited about this new opportunity, I told Roy as soon as he came home from work. He said "We can't take it on" but I was determined and had held the purse strings since moving to Snape Hill Lane. I went into my 'immovable mode' and made enquiries about buying it. I made a 'For Sale' notice for our front and had several enquiries, but from people in a chain. I felt that would not be a problem and God helped me again in my need.

My mother told her neighbour, Mrs Hoy, three bungalows down, about me wanting to sell. She had a friend who wanted to retire from housekeeping for a gentleman. Mrs Clayton came to view our house and said it was just what she needed. We had had a small bath installed in the kitchen. We had to lift a light worktop and attach it to the wall and a pipe from the gas geyser filled it. The outside toilets were away from the houses. Mrs Clayton was prepared to pay the full asking price of £8,000. Stephen and I walked with her down to the bus stop and then we walked back through Cliffe Park, both full of happiness and praising Jesus for making the way clear to buy our next home, Number 30 Alexandra Road. I have known sheer joy in my life and that was one of the occasions.

With help from my brother Hugh we were able to carry almost everything across the waste land and Dora helped with her car. The new house had a large living kitchen and stairs separating the large front room. There was a big cellar, two bedrooms and a very large attic. With the grant we had the back bedroom divided up for a bathroom and the other necessary improvements. It was compulsory to have a dormer window put into the attic as part of the grant deal. This was another blessing because we could then view Apperknowle and Hundall and the woods.

Although Roy opposed everything I tried to do at the time, he always gave me credit afterwards and he did tell people that "If it had been left to him, we would be nowhere". I agree. It would have been better to have had his support during those times but God was in charge and we can't have anyone better than him.

We had access from our shared drive then passed the door of Number 28 to reach our own back door. Mr and Mrs Smith were very nice. They had two small Jack Russell dogs that were vicious but they quickly became friendly with us and Mr Smith carried them indoors when they barked at visitors. There was a gate and low wall separating us. Our neighbours next up, separated by a wall and drive, had a much larger home. They were

Mr Ralph Hawley, Stephen's PE and geography teacher at Gladys Buxton school and Mrs Hawley was a supply teacher. They were a lovely couple.

I missed the open coal fire and the ovens we had at Snape Hill Lane; here we only had soulless gas fires in both downstairs rooms. Stephen had a dart board in the attic. For the first time, and at Stephen's suggestion, we had a telephone on the stairs wall.

Bernard, Joan's husband, who worked for a carpet and tile store, tiled our kitchen floor and it was lovely. The fridge sat at the top of the cellar under a stone slab, which was very useful.

One day Mr and Mrs Smith gave me a lift home. The two dogs were on a ledge behind my neck as I sat in the back. I was uncomfortable with them being there, fully expecting both of them to be devouring my neck, but it was safe because they must have been used to me. I was very glad to get home. The dogs were the Smiths' children and they were thrilled to have given me a lift with them. Later Mr and Mrs Smith moved into a private bungalow with more access for the dogs to run about and our next door neighbours from the bottom cottage at Snape Hill Lane bought their house.

I had a lovely surprise one day. Stephen brought me a letter from his English teacher asking if I would help serve at a stall for their Spring Fair. I felt very honoured and enjoyed the afternoon working with the friendly teacher. Stephen was really proud of me.

Dora brought Lily to see us and I took Stephen to see Lily. She had moved into a new bungalow on Smithy Croft at Dronfield Woodhouse, as the cottages had been condemned for not having a cellar. Lily didn't like the neighbours and vice versa. It had been the same at Millhouses. Lily had told me about her neighbours rowing but I felt that she was scarcely free from blame herself. Joe, her husband, had died – I never knew when.

When she was younger and slimmer, Lily must have been quite beautiful with her sharp features, big blue eyes and naturally curly hair. She died in hospital when Stephen was 13 years old. Roy then became 'all over us' as they say. I couldn't accept this, for he had deserted Stephen during his formative years and I had suffered years of loneliness. Our relationship continued to be fragile and I felt that his ostensible change of heart was too late.

It was a big shock when my mother died in 1975. Billy, Gladys' husband had died the previous month but this was expected as he had suffered cancer. Mother was on holiday in Skegness with Marie, Raymond and Karen, their daughter. Shaun their son was on holiday in Wales. As expected, Marie inherited the bungalow.

Hugh used to take his little terrier dog up Hill Top, Dronfield to watch the A61 being built. He was fascinated by the engineering and technology. After it was opened on 16 October 1975 he still went up to watch the traffic.

Stephen left Henry Fanshawe School when he was 16 and applied for a job as a storekeeper at Land Pyrometers Ltd. Fifty-two others applied but Stephen was given the job. He worked Monday to Thursday and went to Chesterfield Technical College on Fridays between 9am and 8pm, and he often worked on Saturday mornings.

Stephen was a wonderful young man, tall and with a 34 inch waist, fair hair and with marvellously strong teeth. He had a lovely personality and immaculate manners. He had always been a good pal to me. With the separate lives that Roy and I had lived, I had poured all my love and care into Stephen. But he turned out well and was mature for his years. A lady 'in authority' once told me that Stephen was "the best of the bunch". I was very grateful for her telling me this, after all the years when he hadn't had a dad in his formative years.

He was very proud to give me his 'bed and board' from his wages. I bought him bits and bobs, although once I bought him a pair of trousers I thought he would like, but he looked at them with horror! Thankfully, I was able to return them. Undeterred, a few weeks later I saw a plaid fleece jacket and bought it on the understanding I could return it. He said it was spot on and wore it constantly.

❧

In January 1977 I was at the Dronfield Civic Centre when I saw a notice in Slack's the bread shop saying they had a vacancy for part time work. I liked the look of the shop and the staff, so I applied. I was interviewed by two supervisors, Vivienne and Sylvia. They set me on for Thursday mornings and all day Fridays. I enjoyed the job and having a good memory I quickly memorized most of the prices.

It was a busy shop making sandwiches and selling a wide range of breads, confectionery and cheeses. Messrs Slack had other shops in Sheffield that were also supervised by Vivienne and Sylvia. Mr Slack senior often came and stood watching us working.

Nearing the end of his first year at Land Pyrometers, Mr Tom Land offered Stephen the opportunity of being their first apprentice engineer, making car and aeroplane parts. This was a wonderful opportunity for him and Roy, who was a maintenance engineer, was thrilled. Stephen went to Chesterfield Technical College for a full year, Monday to Friday, and then the apprenticeship was for a further three years, all day on Fridays between 9am to 8pm.

When Stephen was almost 17, a friend told me he had a 'lass' called Jacky. After a time he brought her to meet Roy and me and we both came to love her as a daughter. They were happy together. Jacky's mum came to introduce Mandy, Jacky's younger sister. Ann and Mandy were very petite; Jacky was more sturdy and a bit of a tomboy.

Jacky had come to live with us for free. She took over Stephen's bedroom and he slept in the attic; a pleasant, big room with the dormer window looking out to Apperknowle and Hundall and the woods. It was a good time and Jacky enjoyed the meals I cooked. On Stephen's 18th birthday he and Jacky became engaged to be married.

~

I was asked to do more hours at Slack's and agreed to do Saturdays, thereby working the three busiest days of the week. Then our manageress asked me to cover her Monday afternoons off. On two occasions she rang me in the evening to say that the till was short. This caused me stress but they knew my integrity and the errors were traced. Soon I was covering for holidays and I began to feel that I was neglecting Stephen. He was coming home from work to an empty home and he and Roy had to wait for me to finish the meals, even though I had prepared as much as possible before leaving for work.

On my way home one teatime, I called at the Princess Stores near my home for a shepherd's pie that had been recommended as a quick meal with vegetables. A man was arranging things in the glass front below the counter. Whilst I was waiting to be served he asked me if the item he had put in was visible enough. I was good at displaying and often dressed the window at Slack's. I suggested to the man that if there was anything not selling, he should display it to draw people's attention. Sylvia had taught me that. He then asked me about cheese. I had experience with cheeses as Slack's sold a good variety and used them in their sandwiches.

When it was my turn to be served he introduced himself and his wife as Noel and Vivienne Henri. I had recognized their French accent. They were from

Mauritius. The shop had emptied and Noel told me he and Vivienne would like me to work for them. I asked about the hours and pay. Vivienne explained that she wanted me to cover the evenings because Noel had been getting stressed and she wanted him to have more time to play squash, which he enjoyed and was good for him.

I promised I would think about it, but I knew that the hours would suit me and that I was now working too many hours at Slack's. Noel knew the shop. Also, I thought 'It's nearer home'. I phoned Vivienne to tell her I would start when I had worked my notice at Slack's. When I told Christine the next day that I was leaving, she sat at her desk with her head in her hands crying. I explained that I was needed at home more, and then Vivienne the supervisor came to see me, trying to make me stay but I repeated what I had told Christine.

I enjoyed working at Henri's. I had to get used to selling alcohol but Vivienne was very helpful. Noel was charming and he treated me like a lady. I wore a back and front overall and Vivienne suggested that she and I, and Françoise, their daughter who worked part-time, should wear identical overalls. I went to Chesterfield and bought brown check short nylon overalls with collar and short sleeves. Vivienne gave me the money and asked that when I next went to bring a second set. I did, this time a turquoise blue check.

Françoise and her husband lived in Doncaster and she travelled from there to Dronfield on the train. Noel took her home and stayed in Doncaster playing squash. Noel went to Spain for a few days holiday, leaving

Vivienne and me in charge. On his return he gave me a present of three soaps, two 125g Agua Brava Puig in round containers and one Burley in an oblong case. I had never had such gorgeous soaps and I still use the lovely brown containers for pins, buttons and small items: *Merci beaucoup, Noel!*

Noel asked me work on Saturdays, which I was happy to do, but then on mid-weekdays when Vivienne went to antique fairs. So, I was 'back to square one', spending too much time away from home. I felt I had to leave. They had Jane working for them now so I knew I wasn't letting them down.

୨

The next year Stephen, Jacky, Mandy, Roy and I went to the Isle of Man for a week. I had made Jacky and Mandy two bikinis each, and we had a brilliant holiday.

୨

Ann rented a licensed grocer's shop in Dronfield, where they also made sandwiches. Ann asked me if I would cover for her whilst she went to the warehouse, hairdressers and so on. I enjoyed the part-time work and the pay was useful. Jacky worked there full-time and Stephen helped them on Saturday afternoons.

୨

At the end of August 1980 a man told Roy at Standalls that Jacky had been in the pub at the top of Holmley Lane with a young man. I asked Stephen why she hadn't been there and he told me they were having a break.

Jacky and Stephen came and they stood inside the back door, both crying, and told us they had broken off their engagement. She said that she had met someone else. They left without speaking as Roy and I stood crying. Stephen must have walked her home and then he came back and went into the front room. We knew he wanted to be alone and that he would come out when he wanted to. The three of us were heartbroken. Ann and Mandy were also very upset.

I was quite angry with myself for having let her have Stephen's bedroom, whilst he slept in the attic. I left the shop at Stephen's request but was so unsettled at home, missing Jacky and being unhappy for him. I went back to Slack's and they employed me for the hours I wanted to work: Thursday mornings, all day Friday and Saturday mornings.

Stephen had begun to go out in his car and was staying out late. I nagged him about this because he was working Monday to Thursday and on Friday he was at the College for a long day. He was also taking his final exams and often worked Saturday mornings. As usual, when I nagged he just tapped his nose at me. He wasn't eating and wanted only to go out. He and some of his pals had arranged to go to Spain for a holiday.

Marie had invited Roy and me to go to Yarmouth for a week in September with her, Raymond, Gladys, Karen and her friend Sue and Betty and Arthur, whom I had known since I was a little girl and before they were married. We did not want to go after Stephen's broken engagement but Stephen insisted. Roy and I put on a good face but for me the week dragged, thinking about Stephen being at home on his own. We were very glad to get home and to find that Stephen was all right.

Stephen told me Jacky wanted to come back to him and asked him to give her a second chance, but he had refused and eventually she went to Canada as an au pair. I returned the engagement presents we had been taking care of and after a while I began to use the full set of stainless steel cutlery we had bought them.

Chapter 5

On Thursday morning, 7April 1981, Stephen told me he had a headache. He took two pain killers and went to work but the next morning he said he didn't feel well enough to go to the College and would see the doctor. In the early hours of Saturday, Roy and I were woken up by strange noises. I didn't know it, because I had no knowledge, but Stephen was having a fit. Roy sent for an ambulance and Stephen and I were taken to the Sheffield Royal Hallamshire hospital. Roy followed. After a while we were told he had viral encephalitis and that it had attacked his brain causing extensive damage. He was given a two per cent chance of survival.

Stephen was put on a life support machine after Mr Gumpert, the neurologist, had spoken to Roy and me. I begged him to do anything he could to save Stephen. I remember telling him that I was strong and his answer, that I would need to be.

Roy never recovered from the shock, finding it impossible to accept that Stephen was reduced from what he had been, a beautiful strong young man, taking his final exams at Chesterfield Technical College to be a fully qualified engineer, and now to be like a three year old. We were told that Stephen would probably be doubly incontinent for the rest of his life and would have no memory recall. At home, Roy and I wept silently.

After several weeks Stephen came unexpectedly out of his coma. I was there. He was naked and was moving his arms and legs and I had the strangest feeling for a few seconds that he reminded me of a new born baby. He was transferred to the ward and after a while would sit in a wheelchair during the daytime. He looked so pathetic, with a tracheotomy tube in his throat, skeleton thin and his hair was in four different lengths following the operations on his brain. He had no strength in his limbs and two physiotherapists came daily. Supporting his arms, they took him for his exercises with his legs dragging behind him. It was very hard for me and I was heartbroken, but knew he was in good professional hands.

୨ବ

What caused me endless suffering is that on that fateful Thursday when Stephen wasn't well, I went to work, as I did the next morning when he had said he didn't feel well enough to go to Chesterfield College. He had a headache and said would go to the doctors, so I went to work, just thinking he was overtired from staying out late. I rang him at lunch time and he was surprisingly irritable, unlike him, and saying he wanted to sleep but his dad had also woken him up. When I arrived home he said he still wanted to sleep and I got on with the usual things, washing my hair for work the next day, thinking he was just overtired.

If only I had known, I wouldn't have left him. I would have gone to the doctor with him whether he wanted me to or not. I would have been there for him. This is one of the biggest regrets of my life and all I can do when this still overwhelms me is hand it to God, but every time tears fill my eyes.

Jacky was devastated and rang several times from Canada to ask how he was. I thanked her for the years of happiness Stephen had known with her and for the happiness she had brought to Roy and me. I told her how sorry we were that they had split up, but they were both very young. I didn't tell her that she had brought harmony between Roy and me; it didn't seem right to do so at that moment.

❧

On his 21st birthday, 13 June 1981, the hospital canteen made him a cake and his friends were allowed to visit. Stephen was brought into a large room in his wheelchair but was so ill that they sent his friends home. They feared the virus had attacked again. Thankfully, it hadn't but he was very ill. The Royal Hallamshire staff were beyond praise for the care and support that they showed for Stephen.

One afternoon the lady registrar came to see me, as she often did in passing. She paused to look at Stephen's birthday cards spread out around his hospital bed. Casually she asked me, "Wouldn't you like to see Stephen in a safe room playing with toys?" I was horrified – a safe room playing with toys after what Stephen had been for almost 21 years? I answered quickly, "No, no, Stephen can read". She looked at me enquiringly and in a moment that is firmly etched in my memory, I reached for a birthday card and asked Stephen to read the verse, which he did with clarity. She was surprised and, touching my shoulder, she left.

When Stephen was feeling stronger I asked if we could have him home for a weekend. Knowing the unconditional love I had for him they agreed and a friend took us to fetch him and his wheelchair. When we reached the top of Alexandra Road, Stephen shouted "Stop!". (This was a shock, as he was supposed to have no memory. He hadn't recognized me when he first came out of his coma and often asked who the man was? It was Roy.) This sign of recognition filled me with new life and hope for his recovery. He knew he had come home. Going through the front door he went to the settee where I had placed a protective plastic sheet. He pulled it off and sat down positively.

It was heart-breaking us to have to take him back to hospital and I asked if I could have him at home. I was visiting every day, going on two buses to get there. Roy came in the evening and we went home about 10pm with two big bags of wet washing. This was every day. Roy had bought a Reliant Robin from the same work colleague who had sold him the bubble car. The registrar said "Yes, you can have him home but you will be begging us to have him back in six months' time."

❧

Stephen repeated the same words, parrot fashion, for 22 hours out of the 24. During the day he stood at the front window, knocking on it and repeating the words to passing people or calling through the letter box. Houses had been built on the waste land opposite us so it had become a very busy road. I didn't like him doing this, after what he had been. His beautiful car was on the road at the front. One afternoon a young policewoman came to say that a lady had reported that Stephen had said he was going to take drugs and die. I invited her in so that she could listen to him repeating and she apologized for disturbing us.

Stephen's friends came to see him at first but it was not easy for them and I quite understood when they gradually stopped coming. For a while a pang went through me as they drove past us.

Chapter 6

When Stephen was eight years old Mrs Percy Keebles came past when I was cleaning a mat on the wall at our front in Snape Hill Lane. She said, "'ey Hazel, you're always cleaning your little house, I'm lonely now Percy has died. Will you come and have a cup of tea with me?" I promised I would. As I went down her drive I was thrilled to see a bed of violets, flowers that I love.

After I had visited two or three times she told me she was going to apply for a bungalow or flat as she was finding it difficult to get upstairs to the bathroom. I asked her to give me first chance of buying her house and she promised she would. I knew with Roy's wages and what we had saved we would be able to get a mortgage. The years went by and Mrs Keebles hadn't moved; indeed, she was still there when we moved to Alexandra Road, but I never stopped praying for Mrs Keebles' home and I looked at it every time I passed.

❧

In early January 1982 we returned from the Hallamshire. We then had to attend every two months and we tried to make the 9am appointment as Roy didn't like taking time off. He was a maintenance engineer and also worked a machine. The hospital had instructed me that Stephen should go to bed for two hours after lunch and that I had to stay near him for his safety, as he did not recognize anything.

This particular lunchtime I was compelled in my thoughts to take him around the block. I did this every morning to try and get full strength back in his legs. Up Alexandra Road and down Fanshawe was all he could manage.

At the top of Fanshawe Road, Mrs Keebles' sister-in-law was standing at the gate. Unknown to me she had moved there from Holmley Lane. I asked how she was and then how was Mrs Keebles? She told me she had just got one of the newly built bungalows in Hartington Court on Hartington Road. I said, "She promised me first chance on her home". "Yes, she thought about you but said you have enough on." "No", I protested and doubled Stephen back home, made him ready in his wheelchair and rushed up to see her.

Mrs Keebles said her son Gil had put the house up for sale with the estate agent down the road. Back home, I rang the estate agent to ask how much it was and to say that I was interested. When Roy came home and I told him excitedly about the house but he just replied "You must be daft".

My 'immovable being' took over once again. I stood firm, knowing that had God helped me once more. He had answered my years of prayers: why had I been compelled to go outside that day? It was the first time I had disobeyed the hospital's advice for Stephen's routine. Why was Mrs Keebles standing at the gate? After all, it was quite sunny but cold.

I had saved my wages from Slack's, Princess Stores, Ann's, and any spare money I had, and had invested to make more money. There was a lot of work that needed to be done for the necessities. There would be no grant this time. I was bidding against a couple and the price was going up and up. I prayed and prayed. Then, one Thursday morning at 9am, the estate agent's office rang. "Mrs Helliwell, I have good news for you. Mrs Keebles has withdrawn the bidding. She had promised you could have the house." Wow!

The price was over £2,000 more than I hoped to get for Alexandra Road. I put Number 30 Alexandra Road in the estate agent's hands and it sold very quickly to a gentleman for his daughter who was a nurse, and two of her colleagues.

I hadn't been into Mrs Keebles' front room before but when I saw it for the first time I was absolutely thrilled with the beautiful tiled fireplace in marbled brown-beige with a hint of green and pink. I immediately began planning a gas 'living fire' with logs and coal. The fireplace in the living room was grey and blue in plain tiles but it was lovely when polished up. Again I was thinking about a 'living gas' fire, as in the front room.

One teatime before moving in I came up on my own and stood in the back garden surrounded by Mrs Keebles' bushes. I looked up and saw two beautiful smiling faces at a window of Number 11, across the drive. I guessed it was a mother and daughter. We waved to each other. I was awestruck to think how God could have been so good to me. After praying for Number 9 since Stephen was eight years old and Mrs

Keebles promising me first chance after she got her flat or bungalow, I was actually standing in the garden! We really were going to live here in a lovely house with three bedrooms, bathroom, loft, front room, smaller room and kitchen in a quiet cul-de-sac.

The house has a large garden at the back with a very tall and wide hedge at the bottom. There is a small garden at the front and a drive with a double gate. Mr Keebles had been a builder and he had covered the outside walls with cement made into peaks then painted white, all of which are now still solid but difficult to repaint.

We moved in on 9April 1982, a year after Stephen's illness, and lived in the front room with bare floor boards. Mrs Keebles had left us three oil-fired radiators and I kept Stephen as warm as possible. I had asked the lady social worker for financial help but she could not do so because Roy was on a good wage.

After we had moved in, Margaret and Peter at Number 11 came to introduce themselves. They had a young son, Robert, who always looked immaculate in garments knitted by his Nan, Betty. I loved this family and still do. Betty was a wonderful lady; I 'gelled' with her and, of course, I too love to knit. Betty and her husband Eric lived in Brimington and Betty came to call on Margaret most days. Unfortunately, she died a few years ago and I still miss her, as Eric and her family do. She left a big gap.

Mr Tom and Mrs Norah Ashby came every day, in turn, to bring Mrs Allen at Number 7 home cooked meals three times a day. Mrs Allen was blind and deaf. I popped round to see her when I could. When they had attended to her they came every morning to see Stephen and me.

Mrs Ashby brought me a bouquet from their church, the Wesleyan Reform Church, known affectionately as 'the top chapel', being at the top of Green Lane.

Dora died and this also left a big gap in our lives. Colin moved to Bolsover to be near to Joan.

❧

I started to work on plans for the extension that we needed to the house. I obtained three quotes from trusted reputable builders and went for the builder who promised he would be able to start the work when the job they were on was completed. The plans for the extension were drawn up; it had to be bigger than I had anticipated to take account of building regulations and would therefore cost more. The plans were passed and work began. The workmen were brilliant, very respectful and understanding and they got on with their work while I kept Stephen occupied. The addition of a new toilet was vital for Stephen's care because the existing bathroom was upstairs. A shower over the bath was also vital for Stephen.

We lost the outside access to the back garden and could now reach it only though the extension, but as I later found out, with our neighbours either side, this would not be a problem.

Even with the workmen around and the rooms disrupted, Stephen had not knocked on any windows since we had moved in and he began to improve.

&

At the beginning of July 1982, Mrs Ashby invited us to go their Sunday morning Flower Festival service. I was making a strawberry pie with strawberries from the garden when another beautiful friend, Margaret Mitchell, came to see if we were going to the chapel. This gave me confidence, so we walked up. It was crowded, chairs were put in the aisle and at the front of the church. Mr Ashby took Stephen to sit with him in a chair at the front. Stephen had his braces and the medical people had provided him with a urinary incontinence bag which enabled us to go out and about. I was sitting farther back and Margaret was in another spare chair. I wept silently throughout the service. It was so beautiful and I was also repenting for the years I had lost by not attending church.

Whilst at the Flower Festival at the Wesleyan Reform Church I noticed the wooden pews were beautiful and highly polished. I mentioned this to Mrs Ashby when she came to see us and she told me the wood was grained and varnished by their decorator, John Bennett from Coal Aston. I knew neither Roy nor I could now decorate our home, so I kept John's name in mind. I thought that if we had our doors and woodwork grained and varnished we wouldn't need to have paint burned off and repainted regularly. The less work the better, also it would be a strain keeping Stephen off wet paint.

❧

I had been paying Mr North the builder regularly and he warned me that the price would be higher than the estimate. I had anticipated this as extra, but vital, work was found as they went along but I was anxious as the money was running out. Mr North told me, "Don't worry, we haven't completed the work and some jobs can wait. You are able to live in the house and whilst we have this summer weather we have plenty of other work we can be getting on with." I asked him to do that without Roy knowing.

Our friendly local bank manager rang me. He needed to see me and, knowing my circumstances, offered to come to our house. Thankfully, none of the workmen were there that morning. He explained that we were overdrawn. I asked him to promise he wouldn't let Roy know about my financial difficulties. He knew that I dealt with the money and he promised, telling me that it wasn't an amount to be concerned about and that he was confident we would be financially secure when I had finished paying the builder. However, I would have to pay interest on the overdraft and I hadn't to draw any more out. He quickly had a look round and very kindly told me that we had a lovely home and when completed we would enjoy living in it.

I put every penny I could into our joint bank account. I had to give Roy his petrol and football coupon money. Thankfully he had stopped smoking. Roy had always cut his hair with a comb cutter and I used it to cut Stephen's.

I made hot meals out of leeks and onions that I had grown, with lentils for vitamins and potatoes. It's amazing that one can make three meals from one can of corned beef. I also grew lettuce to make soup and for sandwiches. I made leek and potato soup, which was nourishing with my homemade bread, although Roy would never eat wholemeal and so I made him white. We had porridge oats with golden syrup for breakfast. Thankfully we had Stephen's money but it was another stressful time for me and I wasn't able to sleep.

On Christmas Day, I walked down the garden to get some twigs and berries to put in a vase and I found a small bed of mauve and pink Christmas roses. I can still remember my joy. I hadn't seen these growing and it was as though they were a gift from Jesus. I cut the flowers and made an arrangement. The following Christmas I went to the same spot and was very disappointed there was nothing there. They must have been dug up. I constantly looked to see if they were growing anywhere else, but they had been there when I needed them.

Unknown to Roy, I sold my engagement ring in Sheffield. I didn't get much for it but then it hadn't cost much. It was the only jewellery I had, apart from my wedding ring. I still don't have jewellery, it is something I am not interested in, but I must wear a necklace. I got out the teapots I had bought at jumble sales years earlier and sold them to a lady in Chesterfield market.

Naturally, there were the household bills and the insurance man to pay. We had to have a telephone in case there was an emergency for Stephen but I didn't use it. I couldn't take out a loan because Roy would have had to sign; also he was nearing retirement age.

I know I could have asked members of my family, Hugh and Hilda, to help, but again, something may have slipped out and Roy, being very bright would have picked it up. It would have been another burden for me. I was managing but couldn't have coped with any more stress over money. I knew although I was doing my best with the meals I was preparing, they didn't have enough vitamins for us in the long term. I manually juiced Stephen oranges, as I do to this day.

We had brought the Berber carpet with us, so as soon as work in the front was complete we put it down and it fitted perfectly, stretching into the bay window area. Another blessing was the curved four-seater settee we also brought with us that fitted into the bay window as though made for it.

One Tuesday morning in February it was pouring with rain. I was in the kitchen and looking at the few pence I had in my purse. I began to shake – what if Roy needed petrol for our 9am visit to the hospital? Stephen received a benefit payable on Wednesdays but the appointment was too early to call at a post office. I knew they wouldn't pay us in advance. I could have asked my neighbours but my overriding fear was that Roy would find out what a financial mess I was in and my life would be even more fraught. I prayed hard to God to help me.

I saw a figure coming through the gate and was amazed as it was raining, 'cats and dogs' as the saying goes. My former Sunday school teacher, Miss Barber, was standing at the front door and I invited her in. She said that she wanted to get home after a busy morning as a magistrate at a local court, but clearly she felt compelled to come in. She gave me a £10 note from a fund for Stephen. I was speechless but managed to croak "Thank you". That was God helping me out once more when I was desperate. I weep as I write this. I had £10 for Roy's petrol and also I could buy a bit of fish to make a meal from the man who delivered in our avenue on Tuesday afternoons. This £10 was a one off, so I appreciated God's timing.

႙

In April 1983 Stephen had been exceptionally hyperactive for nine months. The only way I could get him to be still was to put him in his bed at 3pm. I stayed with him in the single bed I had bought for me to be near him when he came home from hospital. When he woke, he was pacing the house again as I was cooking. His illness had made him restless but this was different; I was fearful of him falling down the bare stairs, also he now had a varicose vein running down his right leg and over-activity wouldn't help. He was already on the highest dosage of medication for this over-activity.

One Monday morning when it was pouring with rain, I wanted to take Stephen for a short walk. He was normally able to walk a short distance but this morning it really wasn't fit. Stephen was particularly restless and

I couldn't even get him to stay in bed with his word puzzle book whilst I did my knitting in the other bed.

I shouted at God, "What have we done to deserve this? Give me a sign." The bible is full of God answering with signs. I am very ashamed to admit that after all God had done for us, I was suffering for Stephen being so tormented in his mind. I could only think that we had reached the end. It would have been so easy, Stephen was on very powerful drugs and there would have been enough to end it all for him and me. I knew it was scripturally wrong but I didn't care. I was at my wit's end; Roy was being very difficult and I knew this was upsetting Stephen. I couldn't see any light at the end of a very dark tunnel.

Then my eye fell on 'News and Views', a monthly Dronfield church magazine that Mrs Ashby must have brought me. I didn't buy it myself at that time. I flicked through and my hand rested on the page for St Philip's Church. In our lives we experience moments when it seems the world stops still and this was such an occasion. I rang the vicar, the Reverend William Mason and asked him if he would pray for us. I briefly put him in the picture. I found out later that it was his day off and he and his wife always went out whilst their young children were at school. God was in charge. I weep as I write this.

The very next afternoon Stephen sat, quite still, on the two-seater settee that Mrs Keebles had given us. I sat nearby, not daring to move, fearing if I did he would begin his restless walking again. I never understood why

I didn't ring the vicar to tell him this good news but I gave God the glory and prayed that Stephen's improvement would continue. It was another gift of God's divine providence.

Friday afternoon came and the front door bell rang. I looked through the bubble window and saw a man with a black beard, wearing a 'dog-collar'. It was Reverend William Mason. Eagerly, I invited him in and told him of the beginning of Stephen's healing and that he was still restless but steadier and he did settle down more. We were both crying with joy. He then told me that the previous Friday morning a young lady from the church, Hilary, had been to the Vicarage in Green Lane to say that she was confident God was saying St Philip's should begin a healing ministry. William confirmed this. I apologised again for not ringing him to thank him.

Reverend Mason gave me directions to St Philip's church and I went there on the following Sunday. Stephen was unable to come with me but Roy took him for a drive. They told me later that I was like a quiet mouse creeping into church and creeping out again. In those days I was too tired, physically and mentally, to talk to anyone. Sue Edwards gently cared for me. However, after a while Stephen went with me to the church (complete with his urine bottle!). Difficulties arose again, as Roy didn't like me going to church; was he jealous of the vicar of all things? I didn't give in. I had earlier given up attending church for him but this time my 'immovable self' took over. Roy always refused my invitations to come with us but I continued praying for him.

The Robin Reliant didn't take much petrol and on a Saturday afternoon we went to Bakewell. I was trying to keep our lives normal and I made sandwiches from my homemade bread and lettuce and filled the flask. I made plain scones each day, they were filling and the cheapest thing I could think of. Roy suffered arthritis in his knees and so stayed in the car listening to his little radio, while Stephen and I went walking by the river.

My thoughts were, 'I shouldn't be worrying about what we eat for tea. We should be able to eat the grass and drink from the river as God ordained at the beginning of creation in Genesis'. The words of the hymn came to me and I was certain that it was a promise from God; just hang in:

> *Great is thy faithfulness,*
> *Great is Thy faithfulness,*
> *Morning by morning new mercies I see.*
> *All I have needed Thy hand has provided.*
> *Great is Thy faithfulness, Lord unto me."*

The following Monday afternoon a young social worker, Ian, came to see Stephen. He enquired how I was and I told him about my money difficulties. He said he could bring a food parcel. Fearing Roy would find out I refused and told him God would help. I must have made an impression on him because he rang to say that he had found out there was a new scheme being introduced, the ICA (Invalid Care Allowance), and that I was eligible for it. He brought the form to the house. I filled it in immediately and he posted it for me to

Blackpool. On the Thursday I received a circular letter informing the carers of this new scheme and everyone would begin to be paid in a few weeks' time. I wrote to the Controller, putting everything down and ending by saying that I prayed and trusted he could help me.

On the Sunday evening something went through my body. It began at the top of my head then down to my feet and then back up to my head again. I felt as if I was released from a very heavy weight. I thought, 'I'm going to be alright'. I knew something was happening and I managed to sleep, between attending to Stephen.

Sure enough, very early the next morning a brown envelope was pushed through the letterbox. It was from the Controller at Blackpool with a backdated cheque. The amount was enough to pay off the bank overdraft and to cover the estimated amount for the remainder of the repairs and necessary work by the builders and plumbers.

I went down on my knees, thanking God and sobbing with joy. I took the cheque up to Stephen in bed and told him I needed to run quickly down to the bank. He surprised me by telling me I would have to pay tax. After attending to him, I asked him to stay in bed with his hidden words book. I had never left him before.

Arriving just before 9am. I was the first and a small queue formed behind me waiting for the doors to open. I asked to see the manager. He came out of his office and I gave him the cheque, saying quite loudly, "There, I told you God would help me out". He was surprised! I asked

"May I have some cash, please?" Laughing he said, "Of course".

I ran up Green Lane and home to Stephen. Thinking back, I think I flew. Stephen, bless him, was still in bed and asleep; perhaps it was because he knew it was so important to me that he did. That was the only time I left Stephen by himself.

I wrote a letter of thanks to the Controller, adding that Stephen and I prayed and trusted him and his staff, and his family would receive a special blessing from God. Stephen and I posted this and then we went to Mr Moore the butcher on Greendale, where I bought steak for a meat and potato pie and a leg of lamb. The greengrocer on Hartington Road was closed on Mondays. We called at the Cooperative and I bought vegetables and food. I can't possibly describe how I was feeling and thinking. A whole new world had opened up for me, a new start. It was unbelievable.

Excitedly I rang Mr North and asked him to come when convenient as I now had enough money to complete the work. The telephone was a lifeline if there was an emergency for Stephen. He suffered very bad epileptic seizures through his damaged brain and a few times had been unconscious.

I rang Ian, Stephen's social worker. He was out but I left the message with one of his colleagues, "Please tell him as soon as possible that I have received the ICA cheque, and have paid it into the bank." He rang back and after lunch he came up to see us, telling me how pleased he was to be able to help. I offered him a £5 note to buy a bottle of wine. He refused, saying he wasn't allowed to accept gifts and that he had only been doing his job.

Mr North came whilst Ian was still with us and I told him how the money had come. He was very touched and told me he was very thankful for us and promised he would bring his men back as soon as possible to complete the outstanding work. After Ian had left I asked Mr North for the price for an air vent and a big 'hatch window' with sliding glass in the kitchen so I would not be cut off from Stephen whilst working in there or in the extension, to be put in later when I knew I had the money available.

When Roy came home I told him, "That money came". He grumpily asked, "How much?" but I didn't tell him. But then, he didn't know what a financial mess I had been in, but God did:

> *Morning by morning new mercies I see.*
> *All I have needed Thy hand has provided.*
> *Great is Thy faithfulness, Lord unto me."*

I was off to a new start and have never got into a financial mess again. All Glory to God.

For a while I still woke up repeatedly in the night, worrying, and there were also moments during the day until I realized I didn't need to worry, and then my nerves grew stronger.

ఞ

I organised for non-slip floor tiles to be laid on the extension and toilet floors and for non-slip floor covering in the bathroom. I left Stephen's bedroom, our bedroom, the stairs and hall to be carpeted until after John had finished decorating. I was very careful making sure I had enough money before committing myself. I also always made sure Stephen didn't slip anywhere or fall downstairs. It was so wonderful to see our home gradually being completed but it was even more wonderful that I had the money to pay for it!

❧

I had the bag of marigold seed heads my sister Gladys had given me and scattered them on the garden, thus beginning a great love I have for these flowers. Over the years I have selected them to grow different gorgeous coloured heads. A few times they have grown all over the garden and out of control, but gradually I have dug up or chosen the seed heads from the ones I want to keep. They are wonderful and they still flower at Christmas time.

At that time, St Philip's produced a community newsletter called 'Umbrella' three times a year. Reverend 'Bill' asked me to write a testimony about Stephen so as to encourage other people. A lady who was the deputy matron in Neurology at the Sheffield Hallamshire read the article and recognised Stephen and me. She came to a Saturday evening Praise and Healing service that we then had monthly. She was already a worshipping Christian and joined our church.

Everyone at St Philip's was very kind but I knew some people found Stephen difficult to relate to. I would have been just the same if it wasn't my son and not everyone has patience. We look at those who are brain damaged and disabled and often don't see the person behind the illness: it's like looking in a cracked mirror and only seeing the crack and not the mirror. So I was very God blessed to have someone with us who really understood a damaged brain.

Also, I do like nice pots and in 1975 I was looking at plates in Sheffield Atkinson's sale and an elderly lady came up. I said to her, "Aren't these lovely?" "Yes," she agreed, "but it's what's on them that's important". Well, yes, that's true.

❧

Stephen was still as 'thin as a skeleton' and he had to have braces to hold up his trousers; they were a problem because the clips constantly slid off. One Saturday we set off for Buxton for the first time. It was a lovely run and we stopped at Ashford to see the fish in the River Wye. Arriving in Buxton, Roy stayed in his car as usual, listening to his radio and drinking tea from the flask. Stephen and I had a look at the spring well where there was a queue with bottles to fill to take home. After that we always took our bottles when we went there.

After attending to Stephen's toilet needs, we walked up a hill and came to a shop with windows going around the corner. Men's wear was displayed in the first window and I saw some lovely modern looking trousers which looked as though they had a longer depth to the waist.

The shop was busy inside but I asked if Stephen could sit on the chair in front of a counter. When he had finished serving, a smiling gentleman came – I think I must have looked shy – and asked if he could help. I told him I had seen some trousers displayed in the window that appeared to have a longer rise and how, after his illness, Stephen had problems keeping his trousers up. The gentleman cleared a space on the counter and laid out a pair of the pale blue and a pair of the beige trousers. He measured the depth at 17 inches and as near Stephen's small waist size and his leg length as we could wish for. I was thrilled and even more so when he said they were reduced in their seasonal sale. The gentleman introduced himself as Mr Potter and asked if we were local. When I told him where we lived and how far we had travelled, he asked if we would like a drink. "Yes please, may I have a cup of tea and a glass of water for Stephen?" I asked what other trouser colours they had and he brought out a pair in navy blue. I thought that the colour would be useful if Stephen could manage without his bag for a short time.

A smiling young lady brought my tea in a china cup and saucer. A younger man joined us and he fetched braces with really strong clips. Mr Potter introduced him as his son John. John asked if Stephen would like to try on a pair of trousers. When I explained about the bag he said we could try a pair at home and bring it back if not suitable, but I was sure they would be. John then said that with buying three pairs his dad had given us an extra 25 per cent discount. I had the cheque book so I bought the three pairs of trousers; one to wear, one to carry with us and one being washed and dried; and a pair of the braces. We promised we would return very soon. The lady assistants in the handbag and haberdashery and textile department adjoining the men's store waved to us as we were leaving.

I thought Stephen had had enough by then, so we went back to Roy and set off for home. I was so pleased with our purchases and the price that I told Roy he could have a new pair for himself when we returned! I rang and told a lady assistant how well they fitted and how pleased we were and that we would return.

I then began to feel guilty about going to the shop in Buxton when Douglas Turner in Chesterfield had been so helpful and welcoming to Stephen and me. I decided I would ask Roy to take us into Chesterfield the following Saturday so I could show him Stephen's new trousers and explain how we had come across them.

'Blow me down', as they say! On Monday afternoon Douglas rang to thank me – he had sold a very expensive coat to a gentleman, the husband of a friend, Joyce Newton, who had come to the shop on my recommendation and promised to return! I quickly explained about going to Buxton and getting Stephen's trousers and that I was feeling guilty. Douglas told me he couldn't have matched their price and he would have done the same; he was pleased that Stephen was comfortable. God certainly works in mysterious ways. I never cease to be amazed.

On the Friday afternoon I rang John Potter to tell him we were returning the next day for a pair of trousers for Roy, giving his waist and leg size, and asking if they had pyjamas in Stephen' size, socks to match his new trousers, with soft tops that would not dig into his varicose vein. He was pleased we were returning and told me his dad had promised that, with our travelling all the way to their shop, we could have 25 per cent off everything. I thanked him and said that I was grateful for that. I love a bargain.

I think of that Saturday in September as "one of God's best" and after a steady enjoyable run through the countryside Roy parked and we stretched our legs. After attending to Stephen's bag we had a stroll in the park and Roy said he would sit there listening to his radio and have a drink tea from the flask. I had suggested he came with us for his trousers, saying he could park around the corner at Potters, but he asked me to get them.

John had pyjamas and socks ready – best quality as all their purchases – some brown trousers and a pair in a lovely shade of silvery grey for Roy, so I had both pairs at the price. He told me that when clearing the window for new stock, he had found some towels that had a stripe across them, where they had been bleached by the sun, despite the protection of a green shade and the awning outside. He was saving these for a customer who always bought some. I told him I was interested because I used so many towels for Stephen.

Jenny, the smiling young lady assistant, brought me a cup of tea and Stephen's water without asking; we were grateful. Customers were looking curiously at us and Jenny told them we had come a long way and they wanted to make us feel comfortable. They all smiled at us. John brought the towels, lovely thick and soft, plus facecloths, and told me the price. Stephen and I went happily back to the park with our bags and Roy was delighted with his new trousers – I didn't tell him they had been a bargain.

We often went back to Buxton and I bought birthday and Christmas presents for Gladys: some lovely nightdresses in her style and unbleached towels. Stephen and I go on the bus from Chesterfield or Sheffield enjoying the countryside and we have had two short holidays there after Roy died.

❧

I contacted John Bennett the decorator and he came to see me. I told him I had seen his graining in the 'top chapel' and that I would love him to do our woodwork likewise. I showed him what needed doing. A few days later he came back with the price and, knowing this work would 'last forever', I told him I could manage it and asked when he could start. John was then probably in his fifties and had been apprentice-trained, so when he had prepared all the woodwork he began with his special brushes and cloths to make knots and patterns. It was fascinating to watch and I was thrilled; Roy also liked this work very much. We were very comfortable with John in our home.

When he had completed the work I asked if he could paper one room at a time and he brought me sample books of anaglyptic paper for emulsion. There would be no joins in his papering. He had to break off for other commitments but quickly returned.

❧

"Right, Hazel, I'm off for a walk round the table." John always said that at lunchtime. He was going out of the front door. As I approached the hall I looked up at the ceiling he had papered – the pattern began complete and then tapered off to half. I shouted, "Just a minute John – the paper isn't straight." "No, it's how the house is built, following the avenue. You'll not notice when the coving is up." It's a wonder I didn't give John a heart attack because I burst out crying. "I don't like it, John." I vividly remember he was perplexed. "Won't be long, Hazel," and escaped.

After a few minutes he came back. "Look," he said, "I'm not having you upset. I'll take it all down at my expense and re-do, starting at the other end." "Oh, no, John, I can't let you do that. It looks beautiful, it's me – please leave it and I will get used to it." Doubtfully, he went for his lunch and returned again very quickly offering again to re-do it.

With sewing and knitting I had to have seams straight and this applied to wallpapering and whatever. I knew I had to be more relaxed. For a while, every time I went into the hall I looked up but then I stopped doing it. Poor John, having to cope with me, but he knew I admired him and his professional skills very much from years of decorating.

One thing John was adamant about, he would not paint the outside walls. I remember laughing to myself as I was thinking 'Well no, John, I wouldn't dare ask you to do this mundane work, nor would I be able to afford your price.' John died a few years ago but I feel privileged to have known him and to have his expertise in our home. The woodwork is still immaculate after 27 years, apart from a few scratches with new carpets being fitted. It has never been re-varnished and I still love it. I delight in dusting with a damp cloth and then polishing up with a dry – that's all it takes.

Mrs Allen died. It had also been a privilege to have known her, a beautiful Christian lady. Craig and Linda bought the house and modernised it.

❧

Coping with Stephen's illness and managing my life with Roy was becoming more stressful. In January 1985, for reasons I don't understand, I began to want to eat all the time. I baked all day, ate too much and I very quickly put on three stones. I bought a cheap long black coat to cover me when I went out. To brighten this coat up one day, I borrowed a blue scarf that Stephen's aunty Hilda had knitted for him on her machine with big words in white 'JESUS IS LORD'. As I was putting it on I thought, 'How can I wear this? Jesus isn't Lord of my life. I am comfort eating.' I was immediately healed and went to not eating anything between meals and the three stones quickly dropped from me.

Also, in 1985 with money left from the ICA and my carefully saving I enquired about having a small extension built on to our living room, which was very small. The price was right for a straightforward job and plans were drawn up and passed. As far as possible, it was built before the wall with the window in was knocked through. We lost some back garden, as we had with the original extension, but it was worth it. With the hatch window put into the dividing wall in 1983,

100

Stephen isn't isolated and when I am working in the kitchen I can watch and listen to the television or radio through the window.

John bought the same pattern anaglyptic paper for the new ceiling and walls, which completed the long room. We had space for a big dining table which extends when needed and Stephen has always loved to sit at the table doing various activities or just watching the television. I turn the television round when he sits on his settee.

I bought pieces of roll ends in Chesterfield market and made tablecloths and put lace round as my sister Hilda did. These cloths are still in use daily.

I always had plans for the fireplaces in the living room and the front room and when I could afford it we had a gas fitting to each, unseen under the hearth tiles, and with 'logs and coal' the fires give the effect of real flames.

❧

As Stephen became physically stronger we were able to walk farther. We had often to go up Soaper Lane to the dentist for treatment because Stephen's wonderfully strong teeth had unfortunately decayed. I had to prepare Stephen for a big dog at the house in Soaper Lane that might bark. There were times when we had turn back home or I changed him at the dentists. I bought Stephen black trousers. It would have been easier to use taxis or ask friends or stay at home, but I knew this would never get him used to the outside world. It wasn't easy but with my faith I soldiered on and, with grateful thanks to God and the day carers, after a few years Stephen has become used to noises. Could I care this way for anyone else? No, I admit I could only do it for my son.

On her return from Canada, Jacky rang to ask if she could visit. It was for the best that she only came that once. They all moved from Dronfield but Ann came to our Civic Centre Churches Together annual open air service three years ago and the three of us had a friendly time but I didn't encourage her to visit us.

Chapter 7

In July 1986 Stephen suffered the most frightening change in his behaviour and Roy and I went through weeks of Stephen being violent and hitting us. It was unbelievable that this should be happening to the gentle boy who was bullied at school, the pleasant well-mannered teenager who only tapped his nose at me when I nagged him. He was uncontrollable. We were fearful of him and what he would do, but most fearful for him.

I treated him gently, hoping that my love would make him better. Roy found the situation more difficult and I feared that he might react differently, possibly violently, towards Stephen if I hadn't restrained him. I never left them alone.

When, in July 1981, I asked the hospital to let me look after Stephen at home, they agreed but warned me I would be "Begging them to take him back after six months". I understood what they were telling me but I also know they understood the power of a mother's love for her son. But early one morning I awoke from a dream in which I saw myself clinging with my finger tips to a sheer mountain side, crying "I can't do it, I can't do it." God spoke, saying "Yes, you can. Look how far you have come". Clinging on (I still see this vividly) I looked down and at the bottom there were big rocks. Then I was lifted up, it wasn't far and I saw smooth green fields and a blue sky. I knew that was a promise from God. Stephen would come out of this violent phase, as indeed he did. The last verse of the hymn 'In heavenly love abiding' has since been especially precious to me:

Green pastures are before me, which yet I have not seen;
Bright skies will soon be o'er me, where darkest clouds have been;
My hope I cannot measure, my path to life is free;
My Saviour has my treasure, And he will walk with me.

Mr Tom Ashby, minister and father of a beautiful friend, Muriel Stonehewer, told me when we first met that God never promised skies to be always blue, but that he would be with us. Those words were better than any sermon and I have held these before me time and time again.

૭

I had a Sunday night of vomiting and felt very ill. My stomach had been queasy that morning in church and in the afternoon. Early the next morning Roy sent for the emergency doctor who diagnosed a burst stomach ulcer. I heard him ordering an ambulance and I shouted, "No, no, I'll be alright, I can't leave Stephen". The doctor asked me if I wanted to die. Well, no I. I asked Roy to send for my sister Hilda who then lived nearby. She had been a nurse and she came straight away.

I was taken into the Chesterfield Royal hospital. They used a camera to examine my stomach and they found that I did not have an ulcer but further examinations revealed a strangulated hernia, caused by struggling with Stephen. I was rushed to the operating theatre, where I was given an injection in the back of my hand. The doctor and nurses were gowned and masked. I opened my eyes and said, "Excuse me, I'm not asleep yet". It was my first experience of being a patient in hospital. The doctor said very gently, "Yes dear, we know". I laughed about this afterwards. I woke up in bed in a small room with three other ladies. The nurse told me they had put me with lovely ladies, and they were.

Even so I couldn't sleep for worrying about Stephen and Roy. Roy wasn't used to caring for him; he did not have my patience and he wouldn't have nurses in to care for Stephen. I was in mental agony. The nurses allowed me to sit with them at their station through the nights, knitting.

Thankfully my sister Hilda helped and also a lovely friend Sue Waite, who knew Stephen and his needs and had the necessary patience to care for him. I asked them to not visit me spend their time with Stephen. A friend who had been to visit Roy and Stephen came to see me. She told me that Roy was very tense and her words confirmed my fears.

Bill Mason, my vicar, and his wife Hilary came on the Thursday afternoon, as did Roy. Roy looked at me with a vicious face and said, "He's done this to you". I insisted that Stephen couldn't be blamed for his illness. My gentle Stephen would not normally harm a hair of my head. But I knew Roy had a temper and that he might go home and take it out on Stephen. The scene haunted me, Stephen cowering in the corner behind his chair and Roy hitting him with his walking stick. I had previously had to restrain Roy from doing this when Stephen was attacking us.

With hindsight there are lots of things I could have done. I could have asked the hospital sister to contact our GP to arrange help for Stephen and Roy, not accepting Roy's refusal but over-riding him with authority. I could have asked for Stephen to be taken into care. But I didn't. I wasn't thinking straight. It was my first time in hospital and I was unable to sleep. I prayed to God for help.

The following Monday morning during the doctor's round they said they were sending me to convalesce. I told them I was going home. They understood, knowing that I had not been sleeping and that I was very anxious. So I went home and later at the hospital check-up I was given the 'all clear', although I had to be careful to not lift anything heavy. Our church was amazed.

I took Stephen to Buxton for five days, staying in a small hotel that catered for ill people and their carers. I had stepped out in faith once more and when we went to Ash Green for the routine visit to the psychiatrist, he told me that taking Stephen away was the very best thing I could have done.

Stephen still had to wear a urinary incontinence bag, which must have been very uncomfortable but at least we could go out and about. A few times the bag

Above: Stephen at his Day Group workshop

Left: Stephen at home, reading his Dronfield Advertiser

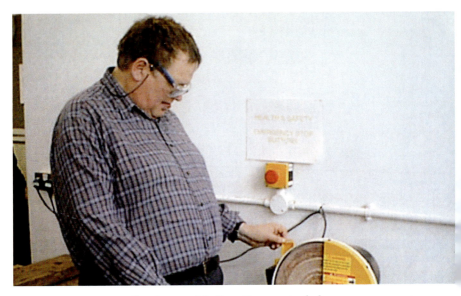

Stephen at his Day Group workshop

*Stephen at his Day Group, making a plant container for
the busy garden at home*

A bracing walk at Ashover heights after Aunty Margaret's birthday lunch. Group to right, L-R, Margaret, Stephen, me

Stephen points out the landmarks at Ashover Heights

The Duchess of Devonshire visits St Philip's Church Feast of Flowers, on 22 June 1990. Canon Derek Palmer offers the visitors book, while Janice waits with the presentation bouquet

Pictured after I had presented a bouquet to the young lady who accompanied the Duchess of Devonshire

The Feast of Flowers at St Philip's Church, 22 June 1990

The refreshment table at the Feast of Flowers;
Janice is facing the camera, Janet is seated, right

The re-building work at St Philip's Church, 1994

St Philip's Church after the rebuilding work

Our beloved Christian Brother, Geoff, at St Philip's Church

Stephen's 40th Birthday; Paul, our Vicar in blue shirt

Stephen's 40th Birthday; Jackie and Simon

Stephen's 40th Birthday, seated with Muriel

Entertaining the party with my home-made turkey 'Tyrone'

Stephen cuts the cake

Above: Stephen shares a joke with Karen and Simon

Left: Anne Ritchie sings, accompanied by Sylvia Holloway

*Preparing for worship at St Philip's Church, Stephen helps
Barbara Stones with the overhead projector*

*Julie Sidey enjoying a display of Stephen's art, pottery
and woodwork, made at his Day Group.*

Enjoying a Church party; L-R, Olive, Jenny, Stephen, me, and Lesley's mother

Roy, pictured at Bakewell in 1990, a year before he died, aged 68

*Gardens are a great joy to us all; I'm pictured in one of my
favourite settings, above in 2003 and below in 2006*

My garden, in the days before writing claimed so much of my time. The upturned orange peel is good for catching slugs!

Left: "I'm not sure about that one, Mum!"

Stephen, about to cut the cake at his 50th birthday celebration

"Arise, shine, for your light has come,
and the glory of the Lord has risen upon you.
For behold, darkness shall cover the earth,
and thick darkness the peoples;
but the Lord rises upon you ,
and his glory appears over you."

I set myself the challenge of photographing the banner that members of St. Philip's Church had made, so that I could transfer it into my computer for the front cover of the Epiphany newsletter. The lettering and cross did not show up very well in the photograph, so I put these in.

It was my Christmas gift to Jesus.

burst, but he gradually regained control and after some time he could manage without it.

❧

Mr and Mrs Ashby died, but their daughter Muriel invites us to chapel tea when it is the annual flower festival and the harvest festival. She also is a beautiful friend and Stephen and I think as her as a beloved sister.

❧

In July 1987 Stephen and I went on a coach holiday for five days to Torquay. Roy took us in the Reliant Robin to Eckington for the coach. We enjoyed the holiday very much with other carers of young men and women with a learning disability. Arriving back at Eckington we were most surprised that Roy was not there to meet us. It was unusual, since he was always punctual; in fact he liked to be early. Stephen and I stood waiting for him and then we saw Peter, our next door neighbour, pulling up with Roy sitting with him, extremely red in the face. I thought, 'Whatever is wrong?' Roy put our case in the boot and I asked him what had happened. Agitatedly, he answered that he would tell me when we got home. Arriving home, the Reliant was in the drive.

Peter left us and after we had gone in Roy told us what had happened. I had left him a shopping list of food we needed for when we got home. Roy had set off to the shop but realised he had forgotten the list. He wouldn't go to our local Cooperative but liked to go to the supermarket at our Civic Centre. For some reason he went a different way the second time and on reaching the bottom of Green Lane the Reliant skidded and overturned on to the roof. Roy got out with help from passers-by. Luckily he wasn't hurt and the Reliant wasn't damaged.

For a long time I had been asking Roy to have driving lessons so that he could drive a four-wheeled car, especially as Stephen relied on us and loved having a run round in the countryside. I also often went with sandwiches, flask and my knitting.

Roy, 'being Roy', didn't want the embarrassment of his workmates knowing he was having driving lessons, although they must have known he didn't have a licence for a four-wheeled car. However, I made the suggestion again and this time he agreed. I think he was shocked by the accident and he knew if it happened when Stephen was in, it would be unthinkable. He took a day's holiday from work each time he had a lesson and passed the test on the first time, a very fine result! He bought a Golf Volkswagen car from an acquaintance.

৵

Stephen and I often talk about when Roy used to take us to Froggatt Edge on the Derbyshire moors. We used to take the primus stove and kettle to mash our tea which we greatly enjoyed in the fresh air with our sandwiches. Then Stephen and I would walk along the path whilst Roy rested.

When Stephen's legs and body were stronger, he and I took longer walks. One afternoon we were walking up Stubley Hollow I was struck by an unexpected thought, 'If Lily was alive we could go to her and she would have a good meal ready for us'.

My heart seemed to swell, flooding through me like a great cleansing wave washing everything away – my hurt and anger, my hatred and resentment of her for the years she had stolen from us with her possessiveness of Roy, causing him to reject Stephen in his formative years, and me. I stood in the lane and sobbed tears of healing. I had allowed God to fully melt my heart into forgiveness and a great weight was lifted from me. I immediately began to feel mentally stronger. I knew that, deep down, although I had previously given all these feelings to God they must have remained in my subconscious, needing to be cleansed.

I felt strongly that I wanted to see Lily and I shared my thoughts with Roy when we returned home, telling him that if his mother was still alive, Stephen and I could have gone to see her and she would have fed us. It was a simple statement, but he cried to hear me talk of his mother that way. He must have known he had neglected us.

One Saturday afternoon in the summer of 1987, Stephen and I were happily delivering the monthly Churches Together 'News and Views' to our customers. We alternated the deliveries, with me waiting whilst Stephen delivered his turn, when in an instant, he disappeared. I ran down the little alley off Bent's Crescent, since that was the only way he could have gone, but there was no sign of him. It was just as though he had disappeared off the earth. I knew it was no good my running after him, for although I was fast he was faster, so I went home, walking in the direction he had gone. Thankfully, when Roy went searching, he quickly found him.

Stephen then began to run off at the slightest opportunity, walking for hours and being sighted always heading for the Chatsworth area across the moors to the Fox House pub. The landlord rang us three times to tell us that his regulars, who had come to know Stephen through photographs, had reported seeing him. Stephen knows the moors and footpaths. It seemed that he never rested and came back as immaculate as when he had set off, but with tired eyes. When he was in the Scouts, Stephen used to go camping at Chatsworth and he hiked all around that area. Walking was what he could do, finding his own way, and it was an escape for him. Naturally these walkabouts caused great stress for all of us, especially when it was pouring with rain and dark.

❧

Mr and Mrs Dengel, who had bought Standall Tools Ltd, invited the three of us to a buffet they had organised for Roy's retirement in 1987. We went to Buxton and I bought Roy a new outfit of beige tweed jacket, dark brown trousers, cream shirt and matching tie and a jacket and matching trousers for Stephen. I already had a two-piece which still fitted me. Mr Joe Hall was there, with all the workmen and staff arranged in a circle. Stephen was brilliant, standing tall and proud.

Mr Dengel made a short speech in which he revealed that Roy had pulled out of a scheme in 1958 so wouldn't receive a pension. He said, "If you had left it alone you would now receive a weekly pension from it and your wife would have a lump sum if you died before her."

Everyone was looking at me. I am very good at putting on a good face but my shock, surprise and disappointment must have shown. 1958 was the year before we married. Roy had a very red face. However, we enjoyed the buffet and the fellowship, and Stephen was very settled and mature.

Roy must have expected me to 'sound off' at him and he was very fussy with me. I had to let it go but the questions remained, why had he left the pension scheme? Who had been given the money? I knew that Roy did not have even the £300 we needed to buy the housed at Snape Hill Lane, and I knew he hadn't spent any money on me. Was it that Lily in her jealousy didn't want me to have the money if Roy died before me? If I had known the facts I wouldn't have married him.

However, what was done was done and thankfully God had provided the means for us. Roy wouldn't have expected Mr Dengel to reveal this personal information in public and he must have been devastated. The men must have seen from my shocked expression that I hadn't known. We all must have regrets. When I am a little 'down', which thankfully is rarer in maturity than in my younger years, I get busy and try to show a positive attitude. I regretted that I hadn't known about the pension scheme earlier, but such is the benefit of hindsight and we cannot change what has gone before.

One thing I am thankful about is when there was talk about Roy staying on longer at work, I told him to retire. I didn't want him under my feet all day at home, but I knew that he had done enough. His brittle bones were suffering from arthritis and his lungs had been damaged by years of heavy smoking. But he had been faithful and a zealous worker at his job. He bought the small Vespa scooter to get to work in the snow and when his old Volkswagen constantly needed repairs.

Recognizing all the mistakes and being reminded of all the lost opportunities in my life, I let each one go, giving them to God. I learned through all my mistakes and fears and I give Glory to God for this.

I think if we had set up in our own home when we married we may have stood a better chance. If Roy, like his brother Joe, had told Lily that his wife and marriage came first, it would have helped. Perhaps, to call on a much-quoted phrase, 'there were three in our marriage'. Perhaps Roy shouldn't have married: he told me his brother Joe always said that he would never marry. Perhaps Joe could see the pitfalls facing his brother.

❧

Stephen had an appointment with, Mr Jamie, a psychologist at the Queen's Medical Hospital in Nottingham. Stephen's social worker, Simon, took us there. The visit took longer than anticipated and Simon had other appointments, so on our return journey he drove fast on the busy motorway, weaving in and out of buses, big lorries, trying to pass everything. I was sitting in the back, petrified and praying that he would slow down and that we would get home safe. I daren't speak for fear of distracting him. Stephen was happy and settled in the front but he was more used to motorways than me. Before his illness he was always driving on the motorways.

As I got out of the car my legs were like jelly. Simon said cheerfully, "If you need to go again I would be happy to take you". I replied, "Thank you, but I never want to travel with you again!" He laughed, "Why not?" "You drive too fast", I answered, "I left my stomach in Nottingham". Laughing again he said, "My mother is always telling me off for driving too fast. I've got you home safely, haven't I?" I thanked him for that and off he went. Thankfully for me, we didn't need to go back!

৯

I am often asked why I did not blame God for Stephen's illness. My reply was always that it was not God's fault. He made a perfect world that it is now full of cruelty and seeming injustice, but those who believe find solace in God's love. I would love to see Stephen happily married – he would be a wonderful husband and dad. My prayers from the bottom of my heart were for Stephen to live. God answered those prayers. I knew his life would be difficult but where's there is life, there is hope.

One aspect I have often thought about is how did I accept Stephen's illness? Was it a throwback to my childhood seeing my mother accepting whatever she came up against? If so, she left me a good legacy with this and that could be one answer, but I know that it was the hope and faith I had in Jesus.

Chapter 8

One Sunday morning in 1987 Roy had been particularly difficult about me going to church and I felt that I could stand it no longer. The morning was a blur. I remembered walking to church with Stephen and nothing more. I couldn't recall speaking to anyone or anyone speaking to me, nor anything about the service. I was in the depths of despair and felt that I no longer cared what happened.

When we returned home, Roy was waiting. I had only just got through the door when he put his arm around my shoulder and said he was sorry for his anger at me! The Holy Spirit must have been working in him. It was the first time he had ever apologised to me. I thanked God and knew that as Roy recognised his need to ask my forgiveness the next step would be to ask God's forgiveness, and sure enough that is what happened. I was thankful for God's grace and was able to forgive Roy.

He asked Paul, our vicar, what he had to do to become a Christian and Paul led him through a six-week course he had devised. It was a searching experience for Roy, and Stephen and I were happy to give him the privacy he needed with Paul.

Paul was in the front room with Roy one afternoon and spoke to me as Stephen and I entered the house. He must have been waiting for us. He said to me, "Now

Hazel, Roy tells me you only cook or prepare vegetarian meals and he doesn't like them and he only likes white sliced bread!" Roy was red in the face and looking sheepish as I replied, "I just think, Paul, that my homemade wholemeal bread helps his arthritis, and I do cook meat – I have a piece of beef in the oven now". Paul said, "Yes, I could smell it". I wondered if Roy had made any more complaints about me but decided to let it go.

Roy completed the six-week searching course, and Paul invited him to give a short testimony at the Wednesday evening fellowship and bible study. Roy was understandably nervous and talked more than usual. Paul went up and stopped him mid-flow. I was hurt for Roy. I knew Roy had been going on but he was doing his best and it was a first for him. I could see he was embarrassed but we were all tired and on the way home I told Roy he had done well.

I didn't sleep very well that night, thinking about the evening before and in the morning I rang Paul. It was on answer phone, so the machine received my rebukes! Roy was astonished to hear me defending him. Later that morning Roy found a letter on the mat from Paul, apologising and explaining why he had had to cut Roy short.

By this stage I knew I had been hasty. Paul was a loving vicar to us and he was wonderful with Stephen, always conversing with him intelligently and with respect; he knew how to draw Stephen out. One day they had a serious conversation about different types of chips. I rang Paul again and apologised for my rudeness and lack of respect, but I explained that the incident had done our marriage the world of good when Roy had heard me defending him before the church. Paul was delighted at this news and the next day came to see us. God works in mysterious ways!

❧

I had two cakes baking in the oven one morning when Roy was reading the bible and he asked me a question. The cakes were burning. I hate waste but this was more important and I answered his question as best I could. The following few years were the best of my life. Roy attended church with us and he encouraged me to hold a bible group at home whilst he took Stephen out in the car. It taught me that one should never ever give up praying for one's needs.

❧

One Thursday evening our church members were going to a church in Maltby for a healing service. It was a beautiful summer evening as we set off, following the cars in front. We went on what I felt was a very busy and frightening motorway and Roy was very nervous; he kept wiping perspiration from his hands. We had never been on a motorway with the Isetta and the Robin Reliant, always choosing the quiet roads to travel on. Soon we lost the cars in front and I asked him to turn off at the first motorway exit. He did, but said "But you want to go to Maltby". I answered that I had changed my mind and that I wasn't having him so stressed by driving there.

The next morning a few church members rang to ask what had happened to us. I told them I wasn't having Roy driving to please me but scared out of his mind. They understood and told me there had been no seen healings at Maltby that evening. But God had worked in Roy and me on the way there.

ॐ

Stephen and I went to the Isle of Man for an organised bible week. I asked Roy to go with us but, as expected, he refused, saying he had things to do. Ken Hallatt took us to Liverpool to catch the ferry. I watched as the big ferry came in and dozens of big motor bikes came roaring out.

We had to go up a wooden plank with our luggage. A cultured lady's voice asked, "May we help?" I looked round and saw the lady and a man smiling kindly at us. They took our luggage and showed us where to sit. It was a vicar and his wife. Stephen and I enjoyed the four hour journey and thankfully the sea was smooth. I had a flask and sandwiches and was very content knitting. Stephen was happy looking around and at the sea. The vicar and his wife were waiting to help us off the ferry and we shared a taxi. They weren't staying at our hotel but we met them several times during the week. I learned that this beautiful young wife was suffering cancer.

I thanked God I had stepped out in faith and had booked this week. We both enjoyed being there with loving people. We had the afternoons free and on two full days we went round the island on coach trips and walked, calling in at lovely cafés for a cuppa.

Returning the Sunday evening to Liverpool, Ken and his wife Mary were waiting for us. Mary had brought us sandwiches, cake and a flask of coffee and we ate before setting off for home. It was wonderfully kind of them. Stephen and I had come to know Mary and Ken through our work delivering the Churches Together monthly News and Views for 23 years. I felt that we had an affinity as they were caring parents for their son.

§

Whilst we were away, Roy had painted the inside walls of our extension with oil-based emulsion. A neighbour came to see how he was. She told me Roy had said he wanted to please me by making a good job of it. I appreciated her telling me that. I don't know why I bought this oil based emulsion, it had been very difficult for Roy to put on and ordinary silk emulsion would have done just as well. Roy was house proud, clean and tidy and Stephen is the same.

Roy could also be humorous. He knew I admired Clark Gable and he used to walk around, mimicking him and holding his ears out! One day I asked him why he didn't buy me flowers. His answer was, "But I do – plain and self-raising". Oh well, I grew flowers in the garden and it wouldn't have made sense to buy more of them from a shop.

Roy was really a kind man but not emotionally strong. In the last three years of his life we were happy together. It could have been like that for our 32 years. I never wanted Stephen to be an only child and we could have had more children. So many lost, lonely years and so much heartache and unhappiness.

What makes you stay when your world falls apart? What makes you stay when hope fails? For me, it was by keeping faith and hope in Jesus and never forgetting how he always helped in other situations.

ఞ

In June 1990 all of the participating churches and chapels in our district held the annual Feast of Flowers and the then Duchess of Devonshire visited each one.

With my heading up the weekend's refreshments, I was asked to present a bouquet to the young lady who accompanied the Duchess. Janice Bancroft in her role as church warden presented the bouquet to the Duchess (the photograph in the plate section also shows Cannon Derek Palmer).

ఞ

In October 1990 Roy was waiting for a hip replacement operation. He had willingly agreed to have a small prayer group in our home but one Wednesday evening he was in such pain that he took to the single bed that I had bought to be with Stephen when he came home from hospital. Roy slept in our front room so that he would not disturb us during the night. He suffered from cramp and had to get up until it had gone. He had a flask of tea and he would listen to his small radio when he couldn't sleep.

That evening our prayer group was in our dining-living room and we prayed for Roy. When our friends went in to say goodnight, he asked if we had been praying for him because his pain had left him. We gave thanks to God for this and prayed for his continued healing. It seemed incredible that after his life of unbelief, Roy recognized that prayers to God could work.

❧

One Monday morning in early December 1990 Stephen was going to his group with his carer when he suddenly disappeared. He was still missing after 30 hours and we were very worried. Roy wasn't well enough to drive. Barry Bancroft came to our house from work as he couldn't settle. The police announced Stephen's disappearance on Radio Sheffield and they wanted our permission to put his picture on Look North and Calendar. I worried that Stephen was so vulnerable and the request filled me with dread. I refused. Our friends went out in their cars to look for him. I couldn't be still and I cleaned and polished, ever trusting God to keep him safe.

On the Tuesday evening I began to realise that we must agree to have Stephen's photograph and an appeal put out on the local television networks. Then just after 8pm Simon, Stephen's social worker, telephoned to say that we would be getting good news very soon but he rang off before I could ask him to explain. The phone rang immediately after I had put down and it was Sheffield police to say they had found Stephen. I wept then as I do now when I think of that dreadful time.

Stephen had been seen on Maltravers Road on the Sheffield Manor estate, where there had had a spate of burglaries. The residents, seeing Stephen wandering about, thought he was a burglar and rang the police. In fact, Stephen was heading for the Royal Hallamshire hospital where he had walked once before.

I asked the policeman if Stephen was all right. He replied, "Yes, he's fine. We've cleaned him up a bit". I could hear Stephen chattering in the background and there has never before or since been a sweeter sound. I was so relieved to hear his voice.

Fred, who had a connection with the police, fetched him. Stephen came into the house, wearing his cap and with a crease in his trousers as if he had not sat down since we last saw him. His eyes were very tired. Our home was full of people and we gave thanks to God for his safe return.

Stephen hadn't been hurt and thankfully I wasn't tested in my faith. If he had he been hurt or worse, I don't know how I could have accepted it. A service of Thanksgiving was organised by our church.

Chapter 9

Our friend Daisy Thompson was with Roy on the first Saturday afternoon in January 1991, when he told her about a pain in his arm. That night he became very ill and I sent for the emergency doctor. He came to our front door and asked, "Have you got a dog?", to which I answered "No, come in", but he persisted, "Are you sure you haven't a dog?" I assured him we had not and that Sasha was next door, so he came in. He examined Roy and left him a few tablets.

During Sunday afternoon Roy became worse, hallucinating and seeing water on the ceiling and other visions. It became so frightening that I rang Barrie, the leader of our prayer group. He and his wife Janice came to the house. Janice was a doctor's receptionist and she recognized the hallucinations were the side effect of the medication.

Our GP came the next morning to find that Roy had stabilised. He gave me instructions to keep Roy in bed and to give him plenty of fluids. Andy came and took Stephen for a walk. By late afternoon Roy was very ill and drenched in perspiration. I rang the surgery again and the doctor came very shortly afterwards. After examining Roy he led me into the hall and told me that Roy had developed double pneumonia and was in grave danger. I was increasingly anxious as the doctor tried for nearly an hour to get Roy into hospital. Eventually an ambulance came to take Roy into Chesterfield Royal hospital. I rang Paul our vicar to set up our prayer chain.

As I was with Roy at the hospital one afternoon, ready to leave to get back home for Stephen, Roy wasn't at all well. Paul was away on holiday and as I set off down the long corridor I thought, 'When I get home I'll ring Reverend Garlick'. He had a connection with St Philip's. The corridor was deserted but in the distance I saw a figure walking towards me. Coming closer, I saw it was Reverend Garlick. I thought I was hallucinating! I told him about Roy and asked if he had time to pray with him. He told me he was going to see a lady member of St John's church who was very ill, but would then visit Roy. I felt God's reassuring hand. They moved Roy to a side room, knowing that I would then be spending the majority of my time with him.

One small incident occurred when I was getting ready to spend the afternoon with Roy in hospital, and Andy, the good friend, was coming to take Stephen for a walk. I popped upstairs for something and on the way down I called to Stephen, "Nearly ready". There was silence and I was filled again with dread. Sure enough, the top half of the stable door was wide open and there was a stool in front of it – Stephen had climbed over. Fortunately Andy came just in time and caught him running down Holmley Lane.

I rebuked Stephen angrily: "Haven't I enough to do? Your dad is ill in hospital and I told you Andy was coming. You love going out with him." But of course, Stephen couldn't remember that Andy was visiting. I was sorry afterwards because my outburst was unjustified. Stephen was going through another behavioural pattern and I knew that he was maturing, wanting to see what he could achieve by himself. Thankfully, he has not attempted to go off alone since that time. I confess that I wouldn't be able to bear it. I think we all have these times when we need to 'escape' for a while.

᭡

I took Stephen to see Roy. He was lying in bed, weak and incoherent. Stephen stood looking at him, then he picked up Roy's radio ear piece which had fallen out and gave it to him. I only took him that once; I wanted him to see where his dad was and why I had to be away from home. We never know what he registers in his subconscious and Stephen probably would not remember, but I did what I thought was best.

Members of St Philip's church cared for Stephen and one couple arranged for a nurse to cover the nights that I was away with Roy. I didn't know at the time but this was a private arrangement funded by them. I was also grateful that the Social Services helped with day care, providing more hours for Stephen's carer to be with him. I was becoming so thin that the hospital provided meals for me.

Muriel Stonehewer visited Roy twice a week, taking yoghurt to feed him. The members of St Philip's church were most helpful during this time, especially Janice. They organised a visiting rota for the afternoons so I could go home, see Stephen and have a shower. Paul our vicar and my brother Hugh and his wife Barbara and my nephew Andrew were also a great help to Roy and our family. Roy died on Monday 6 March 1991 after seven weeks in hospital. Throughout these desperate weeks, Janice took telephone calls enquiring after Roy's condition. When he died, she felt quite lost.

§

Roy's funeral service was a celebration of his becoming a worshipping Christian. I chose the hymn 'Praise My Soul, the King of Heaven' and the chorus from the Isaiah 43 bible passage, 'Be Not Afraid, I Go Before You Always'. Janice said words in tribute to him and led us into The Lord's Prayer. Unprompted, Stephen stood up and went to shake hands with her. After the service, Andy, the young man friend, took Stephen for a walk in the countryside so that he did not have to be at the crematorium

We returned to St Philip's where Paul's wife Rosie and church members provided the refreshments. I was taken home, where our neighbours Craig and Linda invited me in for a cuppa. They had been to the service.

I couldn't understand why people said I looked radiant at the funeral service. I was mentally and physically exhausted after all those hours spent at Roy's bedside. I'd had very little sleep for seven weeks and long stressful nights of being away from home and Stephen. I suppose that I was so relieved that in his last three years, Roy had turned to Jesus and had committed his life to him. I know that, without this comfort, I would have been questioning how after all the prayers, he was lost to us.

Frances, a neighbour whom I had invited to a 'neighbour service' at St Philip's some years before and who, with her husband and daughter, had become church members, brought Stephen and me a hot meal every teatime for a while until I got my strength back. This was a most helpful and generous act and very much appreciated.

My sister Marie was especially moved by Roy's death and by the funeral service and she asked to be confirmed. She had looked beautiful and full of joy when she had married Raymond but it was nothing compared to how radiant she looked after she was confirmed. It was an unforgettable experience for me.

Mr Jamie, the physiologist from Queen's Medical, Nottingham, had been twice to see Stephen at home and I greatly appreciated his kindness and also that he called to give Stephen his condolence on his father's death.

I often wondered why it took so long for Roy to turn to God and the Church. One reason might have been an innate fear in Roy. Lily had told me of a two spinsters who lived near them in Millhouses in Sheffield who attended church and a weekly bible study. They endured constant persecution from their neighbours for their devotions. I would have loved to meet these two ladies but Lily said they were dead. I pray that they and all who are persecuted for their faith in Jesus have been especially blessed by God.

Lily often told me that her neighbours were always rowing with her. I was not surprised, as I knew Lily was not an easy person to like. I often repented having stopped going to church to please Roy. I should have stood firm and the church would have helped us in giving pastoral care. But the blame rests with me – it was my mistake and it is my loss. Thankfully Roy changed with St Philip's church. He didn't tell me but he must have been very grateful to God for the support of the church, leading him to know Jesus and so to be set free.

I know that I have matured in age and in my emotions and have grown in confidence in myself and God. Only Jesus is perfect and there is no perfect church community: Christians are not perfect, but going to church helps us all to learn together.

It helps greatly to belong to a community of believers. Just as soap operas on television are popular because they provide 'virtual communities', allowing the audience to share the lives of the players, we all need to belong to something. As members of a loving, understanding, compassionate community we have the opportunity to learn to grow to be more like Jesus. I know that Stephen and I gain immense strength by being in a church community. God gives us free choices and one of my greatest regrets is that to please Roy I gave up attending church. Thankfully, I never stopped reading the bible and praying to God and I know he never left me.

৯৹

After Roy died I knew I was at a crossroads. It was make or break for Stephen and me. I had to regain my strength and shattered nerves. Dealing with our finances was no problem as I had done so since moving to Snape Hill Lane, and I had arranged the funeral. I sold Roy's car and light motor bike.

I knew I had to be positive for Stephen's sake and I set about rebuilding our lives. He had had his daily routine broken for all the weeks Roy was in hospital and when I was away most of the time.

I had got out of the pattern of sleeping, so during the early hours of the mornings I worked quietly downstairs. I had every light in the house on but at 1am one night, as I was ironing, all the lights went out! I rang Craig next door, who had told me to ring or contact him anytime I needed help. Craig told me there was a power cut and while Stephen slept peacefully upstairs, Craig and I sat together, enjoying a cup of tea in the candlelight until the lights came back on. I hadn't been afraid. It was just that after spending so much time at the hospital, I felt isolated.

Continuing being unable to sleep one morning Dr Harvey, one of our lady GPs, made an unexpected visit. Someone must have alerted her. She brought some tablets, telling me that they would help me to sleep. I thanked her but said that I dare not take them as I needed to be alert to Stephen's needs. She understood my concern and assured me they were very mild.

Dr Harvey's visit reinforced the importance of my being able to 'switch off' from being active. I asked her if she would give me a few more days without taking the pills, as I was sure God would help me. She was a Christian and understood, but warned me sternly, "A few days, Hazel".

That night I switched off one light and, for the first time I got into the bed that I had put in our front room for Roy. I slept for a few minutes. Over a gradual period I continued to switch off one light at a time and went upstairs to bed. At last all the lights were off apart from my bedroom and I had begun to sleep longer and longer. Then, I got into bed and pulled the cord to switch off my big light. My room was well illuminated from the lamp outside. It was a great relief to have reached this stage without the help of medication. I gave my double bed to a neighbour who had a friend in need and I bought a new single one.

໑

The police did a routine security check of our home, saying that Stephen and I were what they called 'vulnerable', although I never felt in any danger, being next door to Craig and surrounded by our other neighbours. They and the police advised us to have an alarm installed.

໑

My only experience of anyone with a short-term memory is with Stephen, and I know that he likes the security of a routine. It must have been hard for him coming downstairs in the mornings with Roy not being there and his car gone. I needed to be positive and to put on a good face. It is necessary to avoid being insensitive, especially about speaking of Roy in terms that might upset Stephen.

The important thing is that we made and make the best of our lives and Stephen and I had to deal with our bereavement. We stepped out in faith and asked for help when we needed it. If I had my time again, would I marry Roy? If it hadn't been for the last three years I would definitely say 'No'. But I did and though it seems incredible, God must have been with me going to work at Standall Tools Ltd, and I did give birth to Stephen.

I wasn't worldly-wise but Roy was even less so. He hadn't been in the forces. He had told me about an incident one morning when he had been on the bus going to work from Millhouses, Sheffield, where he and Lily then lived, and a woman on the bus shouted at him, saying her son was away fighting for his country and why wasn't Roy? He never travelled on the buses again but went on his push-bike. At school he used to stand behind his brother Joe, who was strong. But Roy became so scared about going to that school he was transferred to a private one. Standall Tools Ltd, as it was called then, was an isolated world of its own. I was always (and still am) a home girl, but I was adventurous and I still am.

Chapter 10

I had two long term insurance endowments due to mature in 1995 and in the previous year I began to plan for an ensuite bathroom for Stephen, to be built on to the downstairs living room extension. It would make life easier for both of us and improve the value of our home in Stephen's favour. I discussed this with him and I always welcomed his thoughts.

Travelling on buses, Stephen and I went to look at bathroom designs and decided on a double shower, bidet, a hairdresser's back wash basin. That would enable me to wash and rinse Stephen's hair and give him a wet shave more comfortably, as well as supervising his vital teeth brushing. Unfortunately, Stephen's illness caused his gums to swell over his strong, wonderful teeth and they had decayed. From 1982 this was a battle for the dentist, Mr Robin Greetham. With fillings, crowns and other treatments Mr Greetham managed to save them, but brushing was vital to keep Stephen's gums healthy.

My sister Hilda gave me cones of wool equal to three ply when she had finished using them on her machine and I knitted Stephen's caps and gloves and other gloves for presents. One day I took Mr Greetham a pair and he was delighted, saying that he did a lot of walking and that he really appreciated them. It warmed my heart. He told me his two young sons worked on a farm at weekends and that they couldn't keep pace with their gloves. I asked, hesitatingly, if he would like me to knit them some and also some short-fingered types. He gave me their hand sizes and every time we went to him I took gloves. Hilda's machine wool washed well.

One day, because I was busy knitting something else, I hadn't any to take to Mr Greetham and his face betrayed his disappointment. Every time I gave Mr Greetham gloves his wife wrote to thank me. When Mr Greetham retired, Dr David Ward continued and then Mr Miles Grout, now Mr Richard Potter and Katherine.

The future prognosis is for Stephen to gradually have implants when his gums are strong enough. He now has a top denture which he wears attached to his few remaining teeth. He can't cope with the lower denture. When he goes to his groups he has a cord attached to his spectacles but false teeth are trickier!

After Mr Greetham took early retirement he rang me to ask if Stephen and I would like to go for a five mile walk that he had planned. He fetched us and we met up with his wife Jane and a small group. A friendship sprang up with Robin and Jane. I have been God blessed with going to their lovely home for meals and collecting eggs from their chickens. I like to think that all this happiness for Stephen and me comes from my knitting simple gloves.

Whilst we were with them I spoke through the computer to James, their eldest son, in New Zealand, and James showed me his young daughter through the 'webcam'. It was wonderful to be face-to-face, conversing with someone in New Zealand! I used this experience of the wonders of computer technology in my first book 'Love Never Fails', writing that Amanda, the heroine, used the computer as a link with her aunt in Italy.

~

We had to have a new church building because rain was pouring in through the flat roof plus a lot of other problems.

The Holmesdale estate was begun around 1959 and the Holmesdale Church Centre on Falcon Road was opened in 1962. It was an extension of the ministry of the Parish Church. It was a dual purpose building and quickly became a community centre for mothers and toddlers playgroups in the mornings, brownies, guides, cubs, scouts, wives, bridge, sports and gardening groups and the Falcon Players in the evenings. This was much appreciated by the new residents who came as strangers from all parts of the country, virtually living on a building site.

In those days, weekends were spent with the family, making homes of their new houses. There was much to do, making a garden, bringing up the children, and the church was a focus for families, establishing a fuller community and spiritual life. On Sundays the hall was converted into a place of worship with a simple altar and a circle of chairs. Although the groups paid a small rent, it was not easy to meet the running costs of the building, but somehow the Lord provided.

The choice of name 'St Philip's' came in 1979 from the then Bishop of Derby, the Right Reverend Cyril Bowles, who referred to the verses in John 12 vv20-22: *'Now there were some Greeks among those who went up to worship at the Feast. They came to Philip, who was from Bethsaida in Galilee, with a request, "Sir", they said, "we would like to see Jesus."* Philip went to tell Andrew and Andrew and Philip in turn told Jesus. This also made a link with St Andrews Church at Gosforth Valley.

The Curate's house, built alongside the church, was increasingly used for small meetings and after several developments to both buildings there was need to rebuild in 1994. The old building, filled with memories of worship and community, was knocked down in a single day by a JCB.

Whilst the rebuilding went on the members appreciated the accommodation and support provided by Northfield School next door and the two local chapels in Coal Aston.

The money for the new building was raised with individual giving without the aid of appeals and jumble sales. After being re-built in 1994, St Philip's was commissioned on 1 May 1995 by Peter, Bishop of Derby.

In 1996 the Church Council, on an Away Day meeting, agreed after prayer and discussion the following mission for St Philip's Church: "We aim to be a Church which shows our love and respect to God, our love and commitment to the body of Christ, and our love and involvement in the community."

Stephen and I went on organised walks set up by Mike Penny, who is connected to St Philip's. After these walks we went to a pub in the area for lunch, and doing this gave me courage to take Stephen to the Devonshire Arms at Baslow and other pubs for lunch. I wasn't used to going into pubs. I am very grateful to Mike for this encouragement.

One Saturday after rain pouring throughout the previous day and night, we were walking down the 'slippery steps' at Chatsworth and I was going down very carefully. I asked one of the men to look out for Stephen when he just ran past me! He had no fear being used to them.

❧

Our plans for Stephen's bathroom were gathering pace. Mrs Keebles had bought a dusky pink bathroom suite with a cast iron bath made by a most reputable firm. It is still perfect today. I had an electric shower installed over the bath, but had to help Stephen in and out of it to make sure he didn't slip.

Stephen and I had been to a Sheffield store to choose wall tiles so we could work round the colour scheme. I was disappointed that in the vast range they hadn't anything that matched my vision of 'masculine' tiles. As we were leaving the shop there was a young man by the door, putting a display of insets of nine tiles on to a swivel. I saw exactly what I wanted! An inset of six white tiles makes a lovely seaside scene. I wrote down the code and price.

Hoping to find the best price for these items, we went to Chesterfield the next day to a tile studio and told them about the Sheffield tiles. I gave them the code and price and the owner said he would ring me. He did and he dropped the price to get my order. Now we had the colour scheme. I enquired about non-slip floor covering and found a colour to match the tiles and Stephen's bedroom. It was expensive but necessary, as it was in the front bathroom.

The ensuite extension wouldn't interfere with Craig and Linda next door and they were happy for it to be built, as were Margaret and Peter. I requested a frosted glass window in the corridor overlooking their home and this was included in the plans. The building regulations stated that two iron girders were needed in the floor which meant damaging the ceiling of the downstairs extension. I had planned in my mind to take Stephen on holiday whilst his bedroom was out of action.

In early summer 1995, Stephen was asked to go for a week's assessment at Ash Green to review his medication. Taking this opportunity I asked the builders I had used before, Gerald Swift, Alfred Dunham's and Mr North junior, to do the work but they couldn't take on during this period, it being summer, so I contacted another company. They knew about Stephen and my needs and they promised to get the major parts of the job done when I wanted. I had booked the local, first class, plumbers who had done the plumbing work for Mr North.

Knowing the disruption that the building work would create, I asked Ash Green if Stephen could stay a further week and they welcomed the opportunity to give him a fuller assessment. They allowed me to visit Stephen every afternoon and I went on the regular bus service into Chesterfield. It was hard for me to leave him at teatime but I put on a cheerful face and said "Enjoy yourself – see you tomorrow afternoon". Stephen was 'cool' as they say!

As promised, the builders came and did as much of the work as they could before knocking through the bedroom wall and window. They put boards across the exposed areas when they left at night because it was quite open to the weather elements. I never felt in any danger and slept well. Also the downstairs room was out of action with the girders being installed. Stephen stayed at Ash Green for a further few days and although the bathroom wasn't fully completed when he came home, we had got rid of the dirt and mess.

Stephen went back to Ash Green later for five days and I wasn't allowed to visit this time. This was hard for me but I spent the time spring cleaning the house and gardening. For a few years Stephen had suffered with a varicose vein in his right leg and an ulcer developed on the lower part of his leg. I hadn't seen an ulcer previously and this was deep and big. The district nurses came three times a week to check and dress it.

Ash Green had said I needn't send any dressings as they had supplies but on the Friday lunchtime a lady telephoned me to say that they had run out of dressings and enquired if I would be in later that afternoon? I told her I would be in.

A smiling lady came and I saw a mini bus outside. As I looked at it I saw Stephen sitting at the back of the vehicle. I thought I was seeing things! I asked "Is that Stephen?" Smiling she told me "Yes, we are going for a run in the countryside. Come and wave to him." I went to the gate and the nurse got in. After waving with the others, Stephen sat back and folded his arms as the bus reversed down the avenue. Well, I couldn't believe it! I had been so anxious about him, but it taught me a lesson. I went back inside and made a pot of tea and sat down. I realized this 'visit' was a calculated part of Stephen's therapy. He didn't go again after these five days as he was 'too well', praise Jesus.

The ulcer took ages to heal and left the surrounding area vulnerable to knocks. So, it was no swimming, football or cricket and leg up as much as possible. He has been to a respite care home in Eckington several times as part of his therapy. We go twice yearly to the physiatrist to ensure Stephen is all right and to adjust his medication.

ജ

A young lady physiologist, Emma, came to our home for six weekly sessions. I told her of Stephen's life from his being born, his schooldays and teenage years up to his illness in 1981. I found it very emotional but sensitively and expertly she led me through. When she completed the assessment, she asked if she could help me in any way. I told her about the scene of Roy hitting Stephen with his walking stick, which still haunted me. She told me that every time the ugliness came into my mind, I should think of a beautiful time in my life, a scene or a memory which was precious to me. I began to think of a time when I was beside a beautiful lake. Nonetheless, I have never forgotten this frightening scene, however many times I have given it to God for his healing. It probably has a connection with my childhood and I find that it is fading. Also, I knew Roy wouldn't really harm Stephen, but it was the circumstances and Roy's nervous system.

I told Emma the words Stephen had repeated, parrot fashion, for 22 hours a day, and about his knocking on the window and calling through the letterbox to passers-by. I said that these events had happened at Alexandra Road and that he hadn't done it once since moving from there. I asked Emma why this was. She explained that when Stephen came here to live he left the past behind and it was a new beginning for him. I wept as Emma told me this and her words so encouraged me that all the trauma of getting this home, all the worry and sleepless nights through lack of money, all the upset during the building works, everything had been worthwhile for this revelation alone. All Glory to Jesus.

❧

Severe brain damage caused Stephen to go through various behaviour patterns. His behaviour at Alexandra Road was, it seemed, typical of his condition. He had constantly to check that the lights and plugs were

141

switched off, and had always to make sure the toilet seats were down so they would not bang. Stephen was unable to bear noises, which would trigger an epileptic fit. Roy had to disconnect the doorbells; we had to have a soft tone telephone that switched off; I had to ask people not to 'beep' us as they were passing in their cars, and so on and so on. Caring for someone with a short term memory demands great patience and constant vigilance.

Chapter 11

I had contacted John Bennett to tell him what I would need and he told me the downstairs room ceiling paper was obsolete also the walls that had suffered. It was a shame to disturb the ceiling in the original part of this room and also there was the cost for this. I had enough money for extra work but I hate waste. Stephen and I went to several shops enquiring for these papers and managed to get the matching ceiling paper quite locally in Abbey Dale.

The young man who did the wall tiling made a wonderful job, to my design of two insets with several scene single tiles, all carefully placed. We could have had help from the social services towards the shower but it would have been their design and I wanted to give Stephen more space to move.

What hadn't been allocated in the price was for a partition separating the bedroom and bathroom. We were waiting for it to be completed before this could be planned. It was suggested that a partial partition be put across Stephen's bedroom at the side of the shower unit, leaving the bathroom open. I told them I wanted a partition also part way down the side of the corridor for his privacy. I was warned that the special frosted and shatterproof material would cost 'an arm and a leg'. Also, it would make Stephen's bedroom dark.

I stood at the bathroom window overlooking our garden studying how a partition could be put in without making Stephen's bedroom dark. Wrestling with the problem, I could see that if we had the top facing partition they had suggested, using full length 100 per cent shatterproof toughened Perspex, but had only the top half of the partition at the corridor side, the light from the window would still shine through and the small frosted window would allow light into the bedroom. Another blessing was with the wood having a pattern and knots, John only had to varnish it and the window sill. The outside walls were plastered later, matching up with the house, before being painted.

For 15 years at the time of writing it has been successful and the bathroom is still as perfect as newly built.

ও

A few years ago Stephen began 'joking', making puns out of words. It is not as frequent as it was and is not a concern for the physiatrist, who describes it as part of Stephen's personality and probably a legacy from Roy. Stephen is being pleasant and wants to make people laugh. I never let him go past two jokes before tactfully distracting him. He also doesn't know what to say to people but it helps if he is given a familiar opening, such as "How is Sheffield United doing?" or something relating to Emmerdale or Coronation Street, or his hobbies, playing pool and bowling. He only jokes with me occasionally; he feels secure with me and knows that I love him and want the very best for him. I know he is pure in heart. Whenever I hear the hymn or we sing,

"Blessed are the pure in heart, for they shall see God" I know that Stephen is blessed.

ॐ

Stephen's medications were gradually reduced and I thanked God for his mercy to him. Stephen suffered withdrawal symptoms for a while but we lived through them. Apart from the early days when he exhibited a behavioural pattern of violence, I have never had any problems. He is a joy to me and a good pal and we enjoy each day as it comes. We have a good life, making adjustments along the way. I am very thankful that after Stephen being so very ill, we still able to do what we do and go out and about.

ॐ

I began to help our then vicar at St Philip's, Paul Sandford, with the monthly newsletter. The more I could do at home, the better. I typed it out on my typewriter and then Paul completed it at the church office. I then went on to produce the weekly notices.

With more publicity coming from our Churches Together in Dronfield and District, I began thinking I would like to be more creative and make more use of colour in the newsletter , although I knew that it would have to be at my expense. I bought a computer in 2001 and I began experimenting with pictures – and wasted a lot of time!

The greatest challenge I set myself was to photograph the banner that members of St Philip's had made, so that I could transfer it onto my computer for the front cover of the Epiphany newsletter. The lettering

'Glory To God, Luke 2 v 6', with a Cross interposed between the words did not show up in the photograph, so I put these in. For Epiphany I changed the scripture to the first verse of Isaiah 60 (see the banner picture on the last page of plates).

It was my Christmas gift to Jesus. It wasn't perfect but it was the very best I could do and it was produced with love. I think that is all that Jesus asks of us, to do our very best and do it with love.

～

I had a small lean-to greenhouse, but I bought a larger one and grew more plants from seed: vegetables, tomatoes and cucumbers, flowers especially sweet peas, petunias for my hanging flower towers, pansies and the violas that I had developed a love for after Margaret next door gave me some seeds from her plants. Stephen helps me with the watering. I have six water butts to conserve the rain water and two compost bins to save everything for feeding back into the soil. I have divided the garden up to make three deep beds and the soil has built up organically over the years and is good. The perfume from the sweet peas is like no other.

～

Lynne and her family moved to Cambridgeshire when she was promoted in her work as an income tax officer. Lynne worked part time and James their son went to a private day nursery whilst she was working. Two years later Lynne was expecting another child.

Hugh and some other workmen had been offered redundancy, as work had fallen off. He accepted. Barbara, who was head cook at Dronfield Junior School on School Lane, resigned so they could go and live near Lynne and take care of the children. They bought a bungalow. Their moving left a big hole in my life but we kept in touch and they visited. They had been wonderful when Roy was in hospital, visiting and taking me there. Stephen and I had visited them at home and they had visited us. We enjoyed our walks with them. I treasure so many lovely memories. Now the family come up to Stephen and me and we also keep in touch by telephone.

ço

My older brother Albert died on 21 October 1997. Unfortunately, Albert and Bessie separated when their children Malcolm, Enid and Roland had grown up, but they remained good friends and in time they lived together again. Albert should have been a farmer but after leaving school he worked down the pits and then he had a saw mill at the back of the 'Steel' council houses at Unstone Green. He delivered logs and wood with his horse and cart. One day, the saw slipped as he was working on wood that was covered with ice, cutting his fingers and he lost the use of his left thumb. He received an insurance payment for the accident and he bought a lorry and set up making pit props, lids and pimmers. He also sold logs from wood that he collected from several sources. Albert and Bessie's grandchildren are Gary, Paul, Jason, Samantha and Mandy.

Jack had been a moulder on leaving school, before joining the Royal Air Force and subsequently returned to work as a moulder. He died in 2003. He had been happily married to Violet and they had Patricia and Michael.

Our vicar, Paul Sandford, was with us for 14 years before being transferred to Derby. The Reverend Christine Rees was chosen to lead us. Christine brought her vision for an all-age church to St Philips, using words and visual aids so that all ages can understand.

Christine has a husband George, daughters Jessica and Hilary and son Dougal. They are a brilliant, friendly family, who have been brilliant with Stephen, and Christine has always encouraged him to participate. She also encouraged us to have a monthly mid-week 'Messy Church' activity for the community, which includes a bible theme, relevant crafts, a celebration and story and a meal.

For Sundays, Christine and her team work very hard making visual aids from lots of different things, including boxes rescued from supermarkets and a multitude of originally designed items to bring fresh new revelations from the bible.

Hugh died suddenly in 2006. It was a great shock and Barbara and the family are still grieving for him. They were a loving family. I have often regretted not asking Hugh how he felt when we had to leave him behind at Unstone Green. When he was 18 years old he served his two-year National Service in the Army. As he was in St John Ambulance he was enlisted into the Royal Army Medical Corps and served in Egypt. He returned to live with Gladys before coming to live with us at

Number 69 after Mr Marshall died. I have never forgotten how he came in the back of Albert's lorry!

૭

For a few years Stephen and I went on the Sunday Number 181 bus after church, leaving Dronfield at 11.50am, going through to Hartington via Baslow and Bakewell. We built up a lovely fellowship with the others on this bus. We got out at Baslow and went to the Devonshire Arms for a wonderful self-service carvery. The owners and staff become friends and going there was like visiting a loving family, and we loved it. We had few short holidays there and twice stayed over Christmas, going to the local church on Christmas morning. These holidays were very beneficial to Stephen and me.

Unfortunately the bus was taken off. We had local meetings about it and we wrote letters to all concerned, including Natasha Engel our Member of Parliament, but to no avail.

Now the only way to get there is to catch the bus from Sheffield to Hartington that arrives at the top of Green Lane at 9.25am. Hikers use this service. We have caught it several times in the summer but it meant having to miss our church service. Also, the bus doesn't arrive back in Bakewell until 6pm and there is a fear that it will be full. So, Stephen and I and some others catch the hourly bus into Chesterfield and spend an hour there before catching a bus to Wreakes Lane, then walk home.

Stephen and I were disappointed when the stewards at the Devonshire Arms moved on and the place changed. It no longer offers the self-service carvery that we so enjoyed. We occasionally go to Bakewell and Chatsworth Farm shop mid-week.

I found out that on Sundays at 11.30am a Number 253 bus runs through the Holmesdale estate to Crystal Peaks, via Apperknowle. The timings fit with the family service at St Philip's, but when it is communion we have to leave the church early.

This is the only bus we have at 'our side' on Sundays. We catch it with friends and we get off at Apperknowle, going to a local pub for a delicious cooked lunch and then taking a walk, looking over the beautiful Derbyshire moors and meeting horse riders and walkers.

God is good and we love being in Apperknowle and enjoying our meal in a relaxed family atmosphere with new friends. Before these outings, our Sunday afternoons were often a lonely time. Sundays are family times but thankfully we are both strong walkers and travelling on the buses and being in the community is a great blessing to both of us. It has been instrumental in Stephen's progress, especially during the period when he had to get used to noises. We are fortunate to live in such a strong and supportive community.

৯

Stephen's carers keep a diary of their day's activities for the Social Services and for years there has been no problem with him. They write that he is no trouble, pleasant, willing and well mannered, just as he is with me. I wouldn't be without him. As far as possible, he has a fulfilled life. I never dreamed, even with my faith in Jesus, that Stephen would progress this far. I have always been able to ask for his advice and opinions, and have been able to include him. Even his short term memory, which had suffered the most damage, is slowly healing and I pray this will continue so Stephen may have even a more fulfilled life. Our life style may not be everyone's 'cup of tea' but it suits us and Stephen is happy. His physiatrists always confirm that he is 'well fed and happy'.

Chapter 12

Stephen and I have our supper then we watch Eggheads, the brain quiz, before switching to the 6.30pm news. I watch the headlines and then finish tidying the sink. On 10 October 2007 we saw the report that three more of our young soldiers had been killed in Afghanistan. Stephen and I prayed. I was sitting, unable to move, thinking what more I could do: pray harder? Yes. Then I began to think about the possible hurt of the bereaved and I thought, 'I could write something'. People have always told me that I write a good letter. This thought was the start of 'Love Never Fails'.

I knew I had to create a strong character who was holding unforgiveness when she should know better. It had to be a female in authority, so I created 26 year old Metropolitan Police Commander Amanda Dansie. She is a worshipping Christian and has a good home life. Despite her training, she held unforgiveness against her fiancée's commanding officer, Colonel Mark Young, when Andrew and two of his colleagues were killed in Afghanistan. Unknown to her parents, Lord Justice Jonathan and Lady Teresa Dansie, she forbade the colonel to come to the funeral.

Four years later, whilst taking her team out on a drugs raid, they were unexpectedly attacked and four of her young team were killed and she was shot in her right knee. Before collapsing she managed to use her Taser gun on her assailant.

Specialists in London, America and other countries were trying to find the technology to repair the kneecap. An ordinary knee replacement was out of the question because the damage was so severe. In hospital she realised how unfair and wrong she had been to Colonel Mark Young as the same thing had now happened to her. Andrew had mentioned that he lived in Derbyshire. She came to recuperate at her aunt's home in Derbyshire, determined to find Mark and ask his forgiveness. She couldn't contact him through security.

Unknown to her, when Mark left Afghanistan he retired and with his training and expertise, joined the Derbyshire police as an Inspector. He then learned of Amanda's attempts to contact him. He was going to Italy for a few days before he was promoted to Chief Superintendent and then afterwards, but met Amanda and he was accepted as her helper during his leave.

They fell in love, married and lived in a manor house near Chatsworth, which Amanda's aunt, Contessa Sophie Gambetti, had bought her. Amanda and Mark had twins, then triplets and ended with her giving birth to Luca.

୬

My setting for this story just had to be in Derbyshire, in the area around Chatsworth and Baslow that Stephen and I know and love.

One early Sunday evening in September, returning home on the little 181 bus, we were all chattering as we do on the buses. Coming up Baslow Hill there was the most spectacular sunset, grander than I had ever seen before or since. We all went silent in awe and gazed at the absolutely glorious colours – deep reds and golds, yellows and pinks. I can visualize it as I write. Thankfully the bus had to slow down in the traffic. I will never forget this sunset and no doubt it also burned an equally vivid memory in the minds of the other passengers. Surely this was just a hint of the Glory of God?

✀

I chose the pen name 'Samantha' because of knowing Sam next door for the first 20 years of his life, before he flew the nest as young men do. It has been a privilege to have known Sam and the children in our avenue as they were growing up and maturing into responsible, respectful adults, just as Stephen has also matured in age and mind. I also have a lovely great niece in Albert and Bessie's granddaughter, who is also called Samantha.

Later I was very God blessed when a Christian friend told me that Samantha means 'one who listens to God'. I certainly do that. I chose the surname 'Arran' in memory of my holiday on the Isle of Arran in Scotland, when I was 18 years old and when God enabled me to climb Goat Fell in dense cloud.

Creating 'Love Never Fails' was another achievement. All Glory to Jesus. And now there are three more books and this auto-biography. In each of my books there is a thread of the Unfailing Love of Jesus.

On re–reading 'Love Never Fails' in published book form, I knew I could have put so much more into it, and so the sequel 'Unfailing Love' was born in my mind. In this book, Amanda's speech was made more informal, using 'couldn't' instead of 'could not', 'didn't' instead of 'does not' and so on, and cutting out the etcetera's I had used often in the first book. Authors are their own most demanding critics and I am always eager to improve my writing. I spent much longer reading and re-reading my proof of 'Unfailing Love'. In fact I strained my eyes but they quickly healed.

In 'Unfailing Love', Lady Amanda continues to forge a new life as a wife and mother. Dedication and high principles made her a respected and successful SAS-trained commander and now she applies these same qualities to her role in the community and to supporting her husband. The book ends with her giving birth to twins Glynn and Scot.

ᔓ

I have been asked many questions about my books, such as why I placed Italians in the story. The answer is that when I was a young girl, a relative helped me to know an Italian family and I loved them. They were glamorous and I have never forgotten them. My friends laugh about me writing about wines as if I am an expert when they know I am teetotal, but there's nothing wrong with alcohol in moderation. I chose kites for the front cover of 'Unfailing Love' as the family and friends greatly enjoyed this all-age healthy sport, having relaxed fun together. One has to be very careful, for once written and published, a book cannot be altered. For each book I have done very intensive research through the Internet and with our very helpful local libraries.

One day, thinking about a holiday in Newquay, with the sun shining in a blue sky over the bays, my next story 'Jason and Marigold' began to take shape. It is a light-hearted romance set in London and Cornwall. Jason is a barrister and Marigold is haute couture and cordon bleu.

The second sequel to 'Love Never Fails' is 'A New Beginning'. In this book I have taken the story to Ireland. Amanda couldn't ride after her knee injury and so her horse Tarquin goes to a trusted farm where he is a successful stud. The story tells of a new beginning with a horse family business who bought three of Tarquin's foals. As the colt strongly resembles Tarquin, Amanda and her family were invited to see him. Through this a great love is born in the Young family and the Irish family and this not only blesses all of them but also the Derbyshire community.

Out walking with our wonderful friends, Robin and Jane, and knowing he had family in Ireland, I asked him a question that I hadn't been able to answer in my research. Robin gave me the telephone number of one of his nephews, who gave me the answer and provided the gorgeous Irish names I used in the book.

છ

Although I did not neglect Stephen or our home cleanliness whilst writing these books, the garden went to pot. There was no time to grow vegetables, only lettuces and rocket. The dust collected and the windows looked acceptable unless the sun was shining on them. I ironed as we needed.

I always ask Stephen for his opinion and advice and he is a good help. For the books we bought maps and Stephen found me the surfing bays, airports and railway stations. For 'A New Beginning', we found out where the ferries went from and their destinations, and also the airports in Ireland. I regularly ask Stephen a spelling and he is always correct.

❦

A Derbyshire publisher produced 'A New Beginning', supplying through Amazon and from the publisher's office. I was very God blessed with a local artist who worked from my composite to create the front cover. He completed it exactly as I had envisaged, with Amanda greeting Mark from work, eager to tell him about their invitation to the family in Ireland.

Proceeds from this book sale are for our local Dronfield Civic Centre Barnardos, and, in Chesterfield, the Spital Lane NSPCA and Littlemoor Salvation Army.

❦

I shouldn't want you to think that I'm always weeping but when I have received the letters of thanks for my sponsorships of the books and given a real insight into what the funding is needed for, I always feel humbled and grateful that I could help. We were invited to our local Barnardos office to see the wonderful work that they do. We have also been invited to Spital Lane, Chesterfield RSPCA.

But it was and is only possible because YOU buy my books. You still do and so I can still give support where it is most wanted. I always offer a big, big thank you to the readers who buy my books, enjoy them and who give me the strength and encouragement to carry on.

❧

I am pleased at what God has enabled me to achieve. I'm happy being able to support needs. However, I am grateful that people kindly respect my request not to disturb Stephen and me at home. I find that I need the time and space to focus on my writing and Stephen has coped wonderfully with it all, especially since his medication was reduced some five years ago.

❧

We had a grand celebration for Stephen's fiftieth birthday party, attended by over 90 friends who had a connection with him, including our church and those from other churches. I booked the Gladys Buxton school hall and Stephen and I went to see Paul, one of the caretakers, to ask how many the hall would comfortably and safely hold. Stephen remembered everything about the school, having been there between 11 and 14 years of age. Paul asked how many we had invited and he advised me to keep it to a comfortable maximum of 80. It was a disappointment that we couldn't invite more, but as it was held on 13 June, some of our special friends were away on holiday and a few were unable to come through illness and other commitments, so the numbers worked out well.

It was a celebration, rejoicing at how Stephen was alive and healed after his illness and all his suffering.

159

Our local Kuchene caterers provided a finger buffet lunch, which was accompanied by glasses of Schloer. The food and cake were outstanding. Anne Ritchie, who is a beautiful friend and has a gorgeous voice, sang, accompanied by Sylvia, who alternates with Olive playing the piano in our church. We had a Beatles selection, as they are Stephen's favourites, and Anne and Sylvia had composed a very amusing football song.

My niece Lynne and her family had put up balloons outside our home so it was a lovely surprise for Stephen, and they trimmed the hall in Gladys Buxton. They, Barbara, nephew Andrew and our church teenagers were all brilliant helpers, contributing to a most enjoyable party.

As we had requested, people gave money instead of buying presents that Stephen wouldn't use, so we could buy a powerful battery shaver and a sonic toothbrush that he did need. We bought these while 'on offer' and so Stephen had money over, which he agreed to donate to Cystic Fibrosis, remembering that when he was on the life support machine, having strong undamaged lungs helped him to come out of the coma.

෯

Writing my books has opened up a new life for Stephen and me. We did signing sessions at Dronfield and Chesterfield libraries, meeting old friends and making mew ones. We also got to know the staff during my researches and Susan and Emma were especially helpful. I especially loved the Dronfield in Bloom coffee mornings and selling and signing in Dronfield Civic hall.

I was invited to the early evening annual prize giving for the Dronfield in Bloom event. It was so lovely. All the primary schools in Dronfield and District had been invited to enter and seeing these confident young children going up to receive their certificates and have their photograph taken was a wonderful sight for me – they were so young!

I had not expected the moment at the end of the show when Mr John McGrory of Dronfield in Bloom called out "Hazel Helliwell, come on down, we know you are here!" I went down the steps and was presented with the most wonderful bouquet. Being photographed with Town Mayor Philip Blackburn by Mike, the editor of the Dronfield Eye, I was thinking, "I wish I had put some eye makeup on!" The crowning moment of the evening was when I was told by a lady from one of our local garden centres that some of the sponsor money from 'Unfailing Love' had been used to buy daffodil bulbs that had been put into small bags and every child had received one. It was such a loving thought that every child was included and each one had a prize.

❧

These achievements were greatly assisted by Mike, Lindsey, Lorraine and Kat at Dronfield Eye (covering S18 and beyond) and their other publications, Activate8 (covering the Sheffield S8 area), and now Twist (covering S40 and S41 from Whittington Moor to the town centre); our Dronfield Advertiser, Derbyshire Times, and especially Allison who, sadly for me, has been moved to the Sheffield Star; Reflections magazine serving Chesterfield, Dronfield, Matlock, Bakewell and surrounding areas for giving my books publicity and the Peak Advertiser.

ഛ

What of our future? Well, of course this is in God's hands but we enjoy each day as it comes. You will appreciate that I want the very best for Stephen and he has very professional solicitors who will take care of his finances, and oversee him.

I aim to begin growing vegetables again and have bought rose bushes to make the middle flower bed into a rose garden. Stephen and I will continue to enjoy the day trips by coach and going on the buses to Buxton and Derby. I look forward to book signings at Dronfield and Chesterfield libraries and to coffee mornings when Stephen and I meet up with friends and make new ones. And I hope that my readers will enjoying this biography and will continue to support our local NSPCC and Churches Together in Dronfield and District. Then Stephen and I will know that our prayers are being answered.

ഛ

Nigel, minister of our Dronfield St Paul's church wrote in the Christmas Update, "When Jesus had started his teaching ministry he said, amongst many, many other things: 'Do to others as you want them to do to you....' And... 'Forgive and you will be forgiven....' (Luke, Ch. 6)".

Nigel asked "This Christmas, among all the giving and receiving going on, our prayer is that forgiveness will be among the gifts given and received. Forgiveness may turn out to be the largest present you will give or receive. Is there anyone you need to FORGIVE this Christmas?"

Reflecting on this message, I realized that unforgiveness and forgiveness being healed by God is the very heart and the essence of my autobiography. I know that it isn't easy to forgive and forget, but it is possible with God's help.

It was unforgiveness that set the theme for my first book 'Love Never Fails'. I prayed that I had written sensitively. I was so God blessed and relieved when a former school teacher and Christian friend in our church told me that she used to edit books and that 'Love Never Fails' dealt with unforgiveness thoughtfully and delicately. Thank you, Jesus.

We plan that this autobiography will be published as we approach Lent and Easter. Nigel's Christmas message still applies to the season as we reflect on Jesus' sufferings on the Cross, in order that we may have God's forgiveness and all the hope and joy there is to offer on Easter Sunday.

I'm not a preacher and I confess that since Stephen's illness in early April 1981, the Easter season hasn't emotionally been my best time. I've reflected on the spiritual meaning of Easter and of how Jesus suffered and died. The Procession of Witness on Good Friday is very precious to me, as is the joyful service for Easter Sunday morning, celebrating that Jesus is Alive and

Risen and the hope this means for each one of us. I have felt great sadness at this particular time, thinking about Stephen's feelings. He must know he isn't as he was.

I know I am not alone in this and God understands our sorrow when anniversaries make our memories most poignant. Stephen always remembers Roy's birthday on 5 December and always mentions it. We very often talk together about the good times he had with his dad.

I came across an old poem, 'Praise You Father', by Marilyn Ashcroft which expresses hope and truth:

> *Praise you Father, for sunshine,*
> *Praise You Father for rain.*
> *Praise You, Father, for good times,*
> *Praise You, Father, for pain.*
>
> *For if there was only sunshine*
> *The flowers would never grow.*
> *They need the refreshing rain,*
> *They need the winds to blow.*
>
> *If life was only good times,*
> *Our faith would never grow,*
> *God uses the times when we struggle*
> *And when we are tossed to and fro.*
>
> *So Praise You, Father, whatever*
> *You send upon life's way.*
> *For You also send power to conquer*
> *And a love that will always stay.*

I am confident that when I am no longer at Stephen's side, he will adapt. I also know that God will take care of him. I have an expectation and excitement of what God still has for me. I am sure there are other books in me to still write.

I take this opportunity to share one of my favourite bible verses from Proverbs 3:5:

Trust in the Lord with all your heart and lean not on your own understanding ;in all your ways acknowledge him, and he will make your paths straight.

And a very old prayer by Patience Strong:

Matters best forgotten bury out of sight. Never bring resentment out into the light....
Don't recount old grudges. Put them out to die. Sleeping dogs can't bite you, if you let them die.
Every day God gives you make another start. Never let a grievance fester in your heart...
Pass by what affects you – leave it far behind.
Nothing's worth the wrecking of your peace of mind.

The first and last verse of a favourite old hymn:

Lord, for the years your love has kept and guided,
Urged and inspired us, cheered us on our way.
Sought us and saved us, pardoned and provided.
Lord of the years, we bring our thanks today.

Lord, for ourselves, in living power remake us –
Self on the Cross and Christ upon the throne.
Past put behind us, for the future take us
Lord of our lives, to live for Christ alone.

The last verse of a prayer from 'Just For Me' that Miss Roberta Barber (Mrs Moore) gave me in 1945 when I was confirmed:

Just for me His hands uplifting,
I need never be oppressed;
Christ, my Great Physician, giveth
Perfect life, and joy and rest.

Oh, Lord, give me eyes to see
All that Jesus has for me!

And the last two verses in this book:

Prayer changes things – nay, more, it shows
God's estimate of right and wrong,
Fresh courage gives, fresh joy implants,
Till I am strong.

Prayer changes things – the circumstance
That seemed unfortunate or bad,
Must work God's purpose out, so I
Am no more sad.

I make no apology for repeating Mr Tom Ashby's words to me: "God never promised skies to be always blue, but he promises to be with us always."

I have mentioned a couple of the old traditional hymns we regularly sing in our church. I include my beloved 'Be Thou My Vision' and 'Praise my Soul, the King of Heaven', which I used in my trilogy. Stephen and I also love the modern choruses and in Churches Together in Dronfield and District we all have a blend of traditional and new.

I wrote in my first book 'Love Never Fails' about Mark recording the tune 'At Last' to be played whilst he and Amanda signed the register, so that she would hear him in privacy with just her close family members. While watching a light hearted film with Stephen one afternoon, I was very God blessed, for in the film we see the couple's marriage ceremony and, as they walk down the aisle to join their guests, there is the glorious sound in the background of a man singing 'At Last'."

ೢ

I did a lot of weeping as I prepared this book. Sitting in front of my computer trying to type with tears flowing from me, Stephen kept passing me a box of tissues and carried on with what he was doing. That was brilliant.

When I had completed it and as I carefully read my proof I wept again, feeling physically and emotionally drained. I left it alone for three days and when I felt I had recovered I re-read it again making more changes. I began to feel emotionally stronger. It's hard but therapeutic work.

ೢ

On Saturday 20 November 2010 I was at the table top sale in the Civic Hall with Stephen and my books. It was organised by our Town Mayor, Philip Blackburn. I was reflecting on the responsibility of being a Christian and witness, my role as a widow caring for my son, and now as a published author. I thank God for helping me to mature. I hope that age has brought wisdom and understanding.

Not long ago some friends came to a little 'party' and as we were sitting in our front room Stephen was next to the telephone. It rang, he answered and then I took the message and said "I'll switch it off". He said "It's all right leave it on, someone else may ring". Wow! We all thought this was a wonderful development and gave our thanks to God.

I am very proud of how Stephen has coped and how he continues to do so.

&

A Christmas card came from a lovely friend in 2009 and it stands on a table in the house. It bears this wonderful poem by Roy Lessin:

Jesus, The Faithful One

The confidence we have,
The trust we hold,
And the hope we carry
Rest in His faithfulness.
Every promise He had made
He purposes to fulfil.
He has the authority
To accomplish all He has spoken.
His power is limitless…
His character, changeless…
His love, endless!